ISBN 978-1-4400-7634-3
PIBN 10119066

This book is a reproduction of an important historical work. Forgotten Books uses state-of-the-art technology to digitally reconstruct the work, preserving the original format whilst repairing imperfections present in the aged copy. In rare cases, an imperfection in the original, such as a blemish or missing page, may be replicated in our edition. We do, however, repair the vast majority of imperfections successfully; any imperfections that remain are intentionally left to preserve the state of such historical works.

1 MONTH OF
FREE
READING

at

www.ForgottenBooks.com

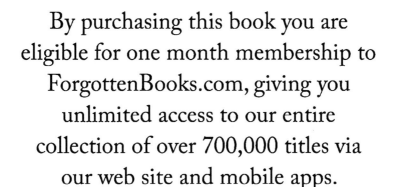

By purchasing this book you are eligible for one month membership to ForgottenBooks.com, giving you unlimited access to our entire collection of over 700,000 titles via our web site and mobile apps.

To claim your free month visit:

www.forgottenbooks.com/free119066

Similar Books Are Available from
www.forgottenbooks.com

HOPES AND FEARS

FOR ART.

BY

WILLIAM MORRIS,

AUTHOR OF

'THE LIFE AND DEATH OF JASON,' 'THE EARTHLY PARADISE,' ETC.

LONGMANS, GREEN, AND CO.

91 AND 93 FIFTH AVENUE, NEW YORK

LONDON, BOMBAY, AND CALCUTTA

1908

UNIVERSITY PRESS:

JOHN WILSON AND SON, CAMBRIDGE.

CONTENTS.

———◆———

003

HOPES AND FEARS FOR ART.

THE LESSER ARTS.

HEREAFTER I hope in another lecture to have the pleasure of laying before you an historical survey of the lesser, or as they are called the Decorative Arts, and I must confess it would have been pleasanter to me to have begun my talk with you by entering at once upon the subject of the history of this great industry; but, as I have something to say in a third lecture about various matters connected with the practice of Decoration among ourselves in these days, I feel that I should be in a false position before you, and one that might lead to confusion, or overmuch explanation, if I did not let you know what I think on the nature and scope of these arts, on their condition at the present time, and their outlook in times to come. In doing this it is like enough that I shall say things with which you will very much disagree; I must ask you therefore from the outset to believe that whatever I may blame or whatever I may praise, I neither,

when I think of what history has been, am inclined
to lament the past, to despise the present, or despair
of the future; that I believe all the change and stir
about us is a sign of the world's life, and that it will
lead — by ways, indeed, of which we have no guess
— to the bettering of all mankind.

Now as to the scope and nature of these Arts
I have to say, that though when I come more
into the details of my subject I shall not meddle
much with the great art of Architecture, and less
still with the great arts commonly called Sculpture and Painting, yet I cannot in my own mind
quite sever them from those lesser so-called Decorative Arts, which I have to speak about: it is
only in latter times, and under the most intricate
conditions of life, that they have fallen apart from
one another; and I hold that, when they are so
parted, it is ill for the Arts altogether: the lesser
ones become trivial, mechanical, unintelligent, incapable of resisting the changes pressed upon
them by fashion or dishonesty; while the greater,
however they may be practised for a while by
men of great minds and wonder-working hands,
unhelped by the lesser, unhelped by each other,
are sure to lose their dignity of popular arts, and
become nothing but dull adjuncts to unmeaning
pomp, or ingenious toys for a few rich and idle
men.

However, I have not undertaken to talk to you
of Architecture, Sculpture, and Painting, in the

narrower sense of those words, since, most unhappily as I think, these master-arts, these arts more
specially of the intellect, are at the present day
divorced from decoration in its narrower sense.
Our subject is that great body of art, by means of
which men have at all times more or less striven to
beautify the familiar matters of every-day life: a
wide subject, a great industry; both a great part
of the history of the world, and a most helpful
instrument to the study of that history.

A very great industry indeed, comprising the
crafts of house-building, painting, joinery and
carpentry, smiths' work, pottery and glass-making,
weaving, and many others: a body of art most
important to the public in general, but still more
so to us handicraftsmen; since there is scarce anything that they use, and that we fashion, but it has
always been thought to be unfinished till it has
had some touch or other of decoration about it.
True it is that in many or most cases we have got
so used to this ornament, that we look upon it as
if it had grown of itself, and note it no more than
the mosses on the dry sticks with which we light
our fires. So much the worse! for there *is* the
decoration, or some pretence of it, and it has, or
ought to have, a use and a meaning. For, and
this is at the root of the whole matter, everything
made by man's hands has a form, which must be
either beautiful or ugly; beautiful if it is in accord
with Nature, and helps her; ugly if it is discordant

with Nature, and thwarts her; it cannot be indifferent: we, for our parts, are busy or sluggish,
eager or unhappy, and our eyes are apt to get
dulled to this eventfulness of form in those things
which we are always looking at. Now it is one
of the chief uses of decoration, the chief part of its
alliance with nature, that it has to sharpen our
dulled senses in this matter: for this end are those
wonders of intricate patterns interwoven, those
strange forms invented, which men have so long
delighted in: forms and intricacies that do not
necessarily imitate nature, but in which the hand
of the craftsman is guided to work in the way that
she does; till the web, the cup, or the knife, look
as natural, nay as lovely, as the green field, the
river bank, or the mountain flint.

To give people pleasure in the things they must
perforce *use*, that is one great office of decoration;
to give people pleasure in the things they must
perforce *make*, that is the other use of it.

Does not our subject look important enough
now? I say that without these arts, our rest
would be vacant and uninteresting, our labor mere
endurance, mere wearing away of body and mind.

As for that last use of these arts, the giving us
pleasure in our work, I scarcely know how to speak
strongly enough of it; and yet if I did not know
the value of repeating a truth again and again, I
should have to excuse myself to you for saying
any more about this, when I remember how a

great man now living has spoken of it: I mean my friend Professor John Ruskin: if you read the chapter in the 2nd vol. of his *Stones of Venice* entitled, 'On the Nature of Gothic, and the Office of the Workman therein,' you will read at once the truest and the most eloquent words that can possibly be said on the subject. What I have to say upon it can scarcely be more than an echo of his words, yet I repeat there is some use in reiterating a truth, lest it be forgotten; so I will say this much further: we all know what people have said about the curse of labor, and what heavy and grievous nonsense are the more part of their words thereupon; whereas indeed the real curses of craftsmen have been the curse of stupidity, and the curse of injustice from within and from without: no, I cannot suppose there is anybody here who would think it either a good life, or an amusing one, to sit with one's hands before one doing nothing — to live like a gentleman, as fools call it.

Nevertheless there *is* dull work to be done, and a weary business it is setting men about such work, and seeing them through it, and I would rather do the work twice over with my own hands than have such a job: but now only let the arts which we are talking of beautify our labor, and be widely spread, intelligent, well understood both by the maker and the user, let them grow in one word *popular*, and there will be pretty much an end of dull work and its wearing slavery; and no man will any longer

have an excuse for talking about the curse of labor,
no man will any longer have an excuse 'for evading
the blessing of labor.   I believe there is nothing
that will aid the world's progress so much as the
attainment of this ; I protest there is nothing in
the world that I desire so much as this, wrapped
up, as I am sure it is, with changes political and
social, that in one way or another we all desire.

Now if the objection be made, that these arts
have been the handmaids of luxury, of tyranny, and
of superstition, I must needs say that it is true in
a sense ; they have been so used, as many other
excellent things have been.   But it is also true
that, among some nations, their most vigorous and
freest times have been the very blossoming times
of art : while at the same time, I must allow that
these decorative arts have flourished among oppressed peoples, who have seemed to have no hope
of freedom : yet I do not think that we shall be
wrong in thinking that at such times, among such
peoples, art, at least, was free ; when it has not
been, when it has really been gripped by superstition, or by luxury, it has straightway begun to
sicken under that grip.   Nor must you forget that
when men say popes, kings, and emperors built
such and such buildings, it is a mere way of
speaking.   You look in your history-books to see
who built Westminster Abbey, who built St. Sophia
at Constantinople, and they tell you Henry III.,
Justinian the Emperor.   Did they ? or, rather, men

like you and me, handicraftsmen, who have left no names behind them, nothing but their work?

Now as these arts call people's attention and interest to the matters of every-day life in the present, so also, and that I think is no little matter, they call our attention at every step to that history, of which, I said before, they are so great a part; for no nation, no state of society, however rude, has been wholly without them: nay, there are peoples not a few, of whom we know scarce anything, save that they thought such and such forms beautiful. So strong is the bond between history and decoration, that in the practice of the latter we cannot, if we would, wholly shake off the influence of past times over what we do at present. I do not think it is too much to say that no man, however original he may be, can sit down to-day and draw the ornament of a cloth, or the form of an ordinary vessel or piece of furniture, that will be other than a development or a degradation of forms used hundreds of years ago; and these, too, very often, forms that once had a serious meaning, though they are now become little more than a habit of the hand; forms that were once perhaps the mysterious symbols of worships and beliefs now little remembered or wholly forgotten. Those who have diligently followed the delightful study of these arts are able as if through windows to look upon the life of the past:— the very first beginnings

of thought among nations whom we cannot even
name ; the terrible empires of the ancient East ;
the free vigor and glóry of Greece ; the heavy
weight, the firm grasp of Rome ; the fall of her
temporal Empire which spread so wide about the
world all that good and evil which men can never
forget, and never cease to feel ; the clashing of
East and West, South and North, about her rich
and fruitful daughter Byzantium ; the rise, the
dissensions, and the waning of Islam ; the wander-
ings of Scandinavia ; the Crusades ; the foundation
of the States of modern Europe ; the struggles of
free thought with ancient dying system — with all
these events and their meaning is the history of
popular art interwoven ; with all this, I say, the
careful student of decoration as an historical
industry must be familiar. When I think of this,
and the usefulness of all this knowledge, at a time
when history has become so earnest a study
amongst us as to have given us, as it were, a new
sense : at a time when we so long to know the
reality of all that has happened, and are to be put
off no longer with the dull records of the battles
and intrigues of kings and scoundrels, — I say when
I think of all this, I hardly know how to say that
this interweaving of the Decorative Arts with the
history of the past is of less importance than their
dealings with the life of the present : for should
not these memories also be a part of our daily.
life ?

And now let me recapitulate a little before I go further, before we begin to look into the condition of the arts at the present day. These arts, I have said, are part of a great system invented for the expression of a man's delight in beauty: all peoples and times have used them; they have been the joy of free nations, and the solace of oppressed nations; religion has used and elevated them, has abused and degraded them; they are connected with all history, and are clear teachers of it; and, best of all, they are the sweeteners of human labor, both to the handicraftsman, whose life is spent in working in them, and to people in general who are influenced by the sight of them at every turn of the day's work: they make our toil happy, our rest fruitful.

And now if all I have said seems to you but mere open-mouthed praise of these arts, I must say that it is not for nothing that what I have hitherto put before you has taken that form.

It is because I must now ask you this question: All these good things — will you have them? will you cast them from you?

Are you surprised at my question — you, most of whom, like myself, are engaged in the actual practice of the arts that are, or ought to be, popular?

In explanation, I must somewhat repeat what I have already said. Time was when the mystery and wonder of handicrafts were well acknowledged by the world, when imagination and fancy mingled with all things made by man; and in those days all handicraftsmen were *artists*, as we should now call them. But the thought of man became more intricate, more difficult to express; art grew a heavier thing to deal with, and its labor was more divided among great men, lesser men, and little men; till that art, which was once scarce more than a rest of body and soul, as the hand cast the shuttle or swung the hammer, became to some men so serious a labor, that their working lives have been one long tragedy of hope and fear, joy and trouble. This was the growth of art: like all growth, it was good and fruitful for awhile; like all fruitful growth, it grew into decay: like all decay of what was once fruitful, it will grow into something new.

Into decay; for as the arts sundered into the greater and the lesser, contempt on one side, carelessness on the other arose, both begotten of ignorance of that *philosophy* of the Decorative Arts, a hint of which I have tried just now to put before you. The artist came out from the handicraftsmen, and left them without hope of elevation, while he himself was left without the help of intelligent, industrious sympathy. Both have suffered; the artist no less than the workman. It is with art as it fares with a company of soldiers before a redoubt, when the captain runs forward full of hope and energy, but looks not behind him to see if his men are following, and they hang back, not knowing why they are brought there to die. The captain's life is spent for nothing, and his men are sullen prisoners in the redoubt of Unhappiness and Brutality.

I must in plain words say of the Decorative Arts, of all the arts, that it is not so much that we are inferior in them to all who have gone before us, but rather that they are in a state of anarchy and disorganization, which makes a sweeping change necessary and certain.

So that again I ask my question, All that good fruit which the arts should bear, will you have it ? will you cast it from you ? Shall that sweeping change that must come, be the change of loss or of gain ?

We who believe in the continuous life of the world, surely we are bound to hope that the change will bring us gain and not loss, and to strive to bring that gain about.

Yet how the world may answer my question, who can say ? A man in his short life can see but a little way ahead, and even in mine wonderful and unexpected things have come to pass. I must needs say that therein lies my hope rather than in all I see going on round about us. Without disputing that if the imaginative arts perish, some new thing, at present unguessed of, *may* be put forward to supply their loss in men's lives, I cannot feel happy in that prospect, nor can I believe that mankind will endure such a loss for ever: but in the meantime the present state of the arts and their dealings with modern life and progress seem to me to point in appearance at least to this immediate future; that the world, which has for a long time busied itself about other matters than the arts, and has carelessly let them sink lower and lower, till many not uncultivated men, ignorant of what they once were, and hopeless of what they might yet be, look upon them with mere contempt; that the world, I say, thus busied and hurried, will one day wipe the slate, and be clean rid in her impatience of the whole matter with all its tangle and trouble.

And then — what then?

Even now amid the squalor of London it is hard to imagine what it will be.   Architecture, Sculpture, Painting, with the crowd of lesser arts that belong to them, these, together with Music and Poetry, will be dead and forgotten, will no longer excite or amuse people in the least: for, once more, we must not deceive ourselves; the death of one art means the death of all; the only difference in their fate will be that the luckiest will be eaten the last — the luckiest, or the unluckiest: in all that has to do with beauty the invention and ingenuity of man will have come to a dead stop; and all the while Nature will go on with her eternal recurrence of lovely changes: spring, summer, autumn, and winter; sunshine, rain, and snow, storm and fair weather; dawn, noon, and sunset, day and night — ever bearing witness against man that he has deliberately chosen ugliness instead of beauty, and to live where he is strongest amidst squalor or blank 'emptiness.

You see, sirs, we cannot quite imagine it; any more, perhaps, than our forefathers of ancient London, living in the pretty carefully whitened houses, with the famous church and its huge spire rising above them, — than they, passing about the fair gardens running down to the broad river, could have imagined a whole county or more covered over with hideous hovels, big, middle-sized, and little, which should one day be called London.

Sirs, I say that this dead blank of the arts that I more than dread is difficult even now to imagine; yet I fear that I must say that if it does not come about, it will be owing to some turn of events which we cannot at present foresee: but I hold that if it does happen, it will only last for a time, that it will be but a burning up of the gathered weeds, so that the field may bear more abundantly. I hold that men would wake up after a while, and look round and find the dulness unbearable, and begin once more inventing, imitating, and imagining, as in earlier days.

That faith comforts me, and I can say calmly if the blank space must happen, it must, and amidst its darkness the new seed must sprout. So it has been before: first comes birth, and hope scarcely conscious of itself; then the flower and fruit of mastery, with hope more than conscious enough,

passing into insolence, as decay follows ripeness;
and then — the new birth again.

Meantime it is the plain duty of all who look
seriously on the arts to do their best to save the
world from what at the best will be a loss, the
result of ignorance and unwisdom; to prevent, in
fact, that most discouraging of all changes, the
supplying the place of an extinct brutality by a
new one; nay, even if those who really care for
the arts are so weak and few that they can do
nothing else, it may be their business to keep alive
some tradition, some memory of the past, so that
the new life when it comes may not waste itself
more than enough in fashioning wholly new forms
for its new spirit.

To what side then shall those turn for help, who
really understand the gain of a great art in the
world, and the loss of peace and good life that must
follow from the lack of it?   I think that they must
begin by acknowledging that the ancient art, the
art of unconscious intelligence, as one should call
it, which began without a date, at least so long ago
as those strange and masterly scratchings on mam-
moth-bones and the like found but the other day in
the drift — that this art of unconscious intelligence
is all but dead; that what little of it is left lingers
among half-civilized nations, and is growing coarser,
feebler, less intelligent year by year; nay, it is
mostly at the mercy of some commercial accident,
such as the arrival of a few shiploads of European

dye-stuffs or a few dozen orders from European merchants: this they must recognize, and must hope to see in time its place filled by a new art of conscious intelligence, the birth of wiser, simpler, freer ways of life than the world leads now, than the world has ever led.

I said, *to see* this in time; I do not mean to say that our own eyes will look upon it: it may be so far off, as indeed it seems to some, that many would scarcely think it worth while thinking of · but there are some of us who cannot turn our faces to the wall, or sit deedless because our hope seems somewhat dim ; and, indeed, I think that while the signs of the last decay of the old art with all the evils that must follow in its train are only too obvious about us, so on the other hand there are not wanting signs of the new dawn beyond that possible night of the arts, of which I have before spoken: this sign chiefly, that there are some few at least who are heartily discontented with things as they are, and crave for something better, or at least some promise of it — this best of signs : for I suppose that if some half-dozen men at any time earnestly set their hearts on something coming about which is not discordant with nature, it will come to pass one day or other ; because it is not by accident that an idea comes into the heads of a few; rather they are pushed on, and forced to speak or act by something stirring in the heart of the world which would otherwise be left without expression.

By what means then shall those work who long for reform in the arts, and whom shall they seek to kindle into eager desire for possession of beauty, and better still, for the development of the faculty that creates beauty?

People say to me often enough: If you want to make your art succeed and flourish, you must make it the fashion: a phrase which I confess annoys me: for they mean by it that I should spend one day over my work to two days in trying to convince rich, and supposed influential people, that they care very much for what they really do not care in the least, so that it may happen according to the proverb: *Belt-wether took the leap, and we all went over:* well, such advisers are right if they are content with the thing lasting but a little while; say till you can make a little money — if you don't get pinched by the door shutting too quickly: otherwise they are wrong: the people they are thinking of have too many strings to their bow and can turn their backs too easily on a thing that fails, for it to be safe work trusting to their whims: it is not their fault, they cannot help it, but they have no chance of spending time enough over the arts to know anything practical of them, and they must of necessity be in the hands of those who spend their time in pushing fashion this way and that for their own advantage.

Sirs, there is no help to be got out of these latter, or those who let themselves be led by them:

the only real help for the decorative arts must come from those who work in them ; nor must they be led, they must lead.

You whose hands make those things that should be works of art, you must be all artists, and good artists too, before the public at large can take real interest in such things ; and when you have become so, I promise you that you shall lead the fashion ; fashion shall follow your hands obediently enough.

That is the only way in which we can get a supply of intelligent popular art : a few artists of the kind so called now, what can they do working in the teeth of difficulties thrown in their way by what is called Commerce, but which should be called greed of money? working helplessly among the crowd of those who are ridiculously called manufacturers, *i.e.* handicraftsmen, though the more part of them never did a stroke of hand-work in their lives, and are nothing better than capitalists and salesmen. What can these grains of sand do, I say, amidst the enormous mass of work turned out every year which professes in some way to be decorative art, but the decoration of which no one heeds except the salesmen who have to do with it, and are hard put to it to supply the cravings of the public for something new, not for something pretty?

The remedy, I repeat, is plain if it can be applied ; the handicraftsman, left behind by the artist when the arts sundered, must come up with him, must work side by side with him : apart from the difference between a great master and a scholar, apart from the differences of the natural bent of men's minds, which would make one man an imitative, and another an architectural or decorative artist, there should be no difference between those employed on strictly ornamental work ; and the body of artists dealing with this should quicken with their art all makers of things into artists also, in proportion to the necessities and uses of the things they would make.

I know what stupendous difficulties, social and economical, there are in the way of this ; yet I think that they seem to be greater than they are : and of one thing I am sure, that no real living decorative art is possible if this is impossible.

It is not impossible, on the contrary it is certain to come about, if you are at heart desirous to quicken the arts ; if the world will, for the sake of beauty and decency, sacrifice some of the things it is so busy over (many of which I think are not very worthy of its trouble) art will begin to grow again ; as for those difficulties above mentioned, some of them I know will in any case melt away before the steady change of the relative conditions of men ; the rest, reason and resolute attention to the laws of nature, which are also the laws of art, will dispose of little by little : once more, the way will not be far to seek, if the will be with us.

Yet, granted the will, and though the way lies

ready to us, we must not be discouraged if the
journey seem barren enough at first, nay, not even
if things seem to grow worse for a while: for it is
·natural enough that the very evil which has forced
on the beginning of reform should look uglier
while, on the one hand, life and wisdom are build
ing up the new, and on the other, folly and dead-
ness are hugging the old to them.

In this, as in all other matters, lapse of time will
be needed before things seem to straighten, and
the courage and patience that does not despise
small things lying ready to be done ; and care and
watchfulness, lest we begin to build the wall ere
the footings are well in, and always through all
things much humility that is not easily cast down
by failure, that seeks to be taught, and is ready to
learn.

For your teachers, they must be Nature and
History: as for the first, that you must learn of it
is so obvious that I need not dwell upon that now:
hereafter, when I have to speak more of matters
of detail, I may have to speak of the manner in
which you must learn of Nature. As to the second,
I do not think that any man but one of the highest
genius, could do anything in these days without
much study of ancient art, and even he would be
much hindered if he lacked it. If you think that
this contradicts what I said about the death of that
ancient art, and the necessity I implied for an art
that should be characteristic of the present day,

I can only say that, in these times of plenteous knowledge and meagre performance, if we do not study the ancient work directly and learn to understand it, we shall find ourselves influenced by the feeble work all round us, and shall be copying the better work through the copyists and *without* understanding it, which will by no means bring about intelligent art. Let us therefore study it wisely, be taught by it, kindled by it; all the while determining not to imitate or repeat it; to have either no art at all, or an art which we have made our own.

Yet I am almost brought to a stand-still when bidding you to study nature and the history of art, by remembering that this is London, and what it is like: how can I ask working-men passing up and down these hideous streets day by day to care about beauty? If it were politics, we must care about that; or science, you could wrap yourselves up in the study of facts, no doubt, without much caring what goes on about you — but beauty! do you not see what terrible difficulties beset art, owing to a long neglect of art — and neglect of reason, too, in this matter? It is such a heavy question by what effort, by what dead-lift, you can thrust this difficulty from you, that I must perforce set it aside for the present, and must at least hope that the study of history and its monuments will help you somewhat herein. If you can really fill your minds with memories of great works of art, and great times of art, you will, I think, be able to a certain extent to look through the aforesaid ugly surroundings, and will be moved to discontent of what is careless and brutal now, and will, I hope, at last be so much discontented with what is bad, that you will determine to bear no longer that short-sighted, reckless brutality of squalor that so disgraces our intricate civilization.

Well, at any rate, London is good for this, that it is well off for museums, — which I heartily wish were to be got at seven days in the week instead of six, or at least on the only day on which an ordinarily busy man, one of the taxpayers who support them, can as a rule see them quietly, — and certainly any of us who may have any natural turn for art must get more help from frequenting them than one can well say. It is true, however, that people need some preliminary instruction before they can get all the good possible to be got from the prodigious treasures of art possessed by the country in that form : there also one sees things in a piecemeal way : nor can I deny that there is something melancholy about a museum, such a tale of violence, destruction, and carelessness, as its treasured scraps tell us.

But moreover you may sometimes have an opportunity of studying ancient art in a narrower but a more intimate, a more kindly form, the monuments of our own land. Sometimes only, since we live in the middle of this world of brick and mortar, and there is little else left us amidst it, except the ghost of the great church at Westminster, ruined as its exterior is by the stupidity of the restoring architect, and insulted as its glorious interior is by the pompous undertakers' lies, by the vainglory, and ignorance of the last two centuries and a half — little besides that and the matchless Hall near it: but when we can get beyond that smoky world, there, out in the country we may still see the works of our fathers yet alive amidst the very nature they were wrought into, and of which they are so completely a part: for there indeed if anywhere, in the English country, in the days when people cared about such things, was there a full sympathy between the works of man, and the land they were made for: — the land is a little land; too much shut up within the narrow seas, as it seems, to have much space for swelling into hugeness: there are no great wastes overwhelming in their dreariness, no great solitudes of forests, no terrible untrodden mountain-walls: all is measured, mingled, varied, gliding easily one thing into another: little rivers, little plains, swelling, speedily-changing uplands, all beset with handsome orderly trees; little hills, little mountains, netted over with the walls of sheep-walks: all is little; yet not foolish and blank, but serious rather, and abundant of meaning for such as choose to seek it: it is neither prison, nor palace, but a decent home.

All which I neither praise nor blame, but say

that so it is : some people praise this homeliness overmuch, as if the land were the very axle-tree of the world ; so do not I, nor any unblinded by pride in themselves and all that belongs to them : others there are who scorn it and the tameness of it : not I any the more : though it would indeed be hard if there were nothing else in the world, no wonders, no terrors, no unspeakable beauties : yet when we think what a small part of the world's history, past, present, and to come, is this land we live in, and how much smaller still in the history of the arts, and yet how our forefathers clung to it, and with what care and pains they adorned it, this unromantic, uneventful-looking land of England, surely by this too our hearts may be touched, and our hope quickened.

For as was the land, such was the art of it while folk yet troubled themselves about such things ; it strove little to impress people either by pomp or ingenuity : not unseldom it fell into commonplace, rarely it rose into majesty ; yet was it never oppressive, never a slave's nightmare nor an insolent boast : and at its best it had an inventiveness, an individuality, that grander styles have never overpassed : its best too, and that was in its very heart, was given as freely to the yeoman's house, and the humble village church, as to the lord's palace or the mighty cathedral : never coarse, though often rude enough, sweet, natural and unaffected, an art of peasants rather than of merchant-princes or courtiers, it must be a hard heart, I think, that does not love it: whether a man has been born among it like ourselves, or has come wonderingly on its simplicity from all the grandeur over-seas. A peasant art, I say, and it clung fast to the life of the people, and still lived among the cottagers and yeomen in many parts of the country while the big houses were being built 'French and fine:' Still lived also in many a quaint pattern of loom and printing-block, and embroiderer's needle, while over-seas stupid pomp had extinguished all nature and freedom, and art was become, in France especially, the mere expression of that successful and exultant rascality, which in the flesh no long time afterwards went down into the pit for ever.

Such was the English art, whose history is in a sense at your doors, grown scarce indeed, and growing scarcer year by year, not only through greedy destruction, of which there is certainly less than there used to be, but also through the attacks of another foe, called now-a-days 'restoration.'

I must not make a long story about this, but also I cannot quite pass it over, since I have pressed on you the study of these ancient monuments. Thus the matter stands: these old buildings have been altered and added to century after century, often beautifully, always historically; their very value, a great part of it, lay in that: they have suffered too almost always from neglect, often from violence (that latter also a piece of history often far from uninteresting), but ordinary obvious mending would almost always have kept them standing, pieces of nature and of history.

But of late years a great uprising of ecclesiastical zeal, coinciding with a great increase of study, and consequently of knowledge of mediæval architecture, has driven people into spending their money on these buildings, not merely with the purpose of repairing them, of keeping them safe, clean,. and wind and water-tight, but also of ' restoring ' them to some ideal state of perfection ; sweeping away if possible all signs of what has befallen them at least since the Reformation, and often since dates much earlier : this has sometimes been done with much disregard of art and entirely from ecclesiastical zeal, but oftener it has been well meant enough as regards art : yet you will not have listened to what I have said to-night if you do not see that from my point of view this restoration must be as impossible to bring about, as the attempt at it is destructive to the buildings so dealt with : I scarcely like to think what a great part of them have been made nearly useless to students of art and history : unless you knew a great deal about architecture you perhaps would scarce understand what terrible damage has been done by that dangerous 'little knowledge' in this matter : but at least it is easy to be understood, that to deal recklessly with valuable (and national) monuments which, when once gone, can never be replaced by any splendor of modern art, is doing a very sorry service to the State.

You will see by all that I have said on this study of ancient art that I mean by education herein something much wider than the teaching of a definite art in schools of design, and that it must be something that we must do more or less for ourselves: I mean by it a systematic concentration of our thoughts on the matter, a studying of it in all ways, careful and laborious practice of it, and a determination to do nothing but what is known to be good in workmanship and design.

Of course, however, both as an instrument of that study we have been speaking of, as well as of the practice of the arts, all handicraftsmen should be taught to draw very carefully; as indeed all people should be taught drawing who are not physically incapable of learning it: but the art of drawing so taught would not be the art of designing, but only a means toward *this* end, *general capability in dealing with the arts*

For I wish specially to impress this upon you, that *designing* cannot be taught at all in a school: continued practice will help a man who is naturally a designer, continual notice of nature and of art: no doubt those who have some faculty for design- ing are still numerous, and they want from a school certain technical teaching, just as they want tools: in these days also, when the best school, the school of successful practice going on around you, is at such a low ebb, they do undoubtedly want instruction in the history of the arts : these two things schools of design can give : but the royal road of a set of rules deduced from a sham science of design, that is itself not a science but another set of rules, will lead nowhere ; — or, let us rather say, to beginning again.

As to the kind of drawing that should be taught to men engaged in ornamental work, there is only *one best* way of teaching drawing, and that is teaching the scholar to draw the human figure: both because the lines of a man's body are much more subtle than anything else, and because you can more surely be found out and set right if you go wrong. I do think that such teaching as this, given to all people who care for it, would help the revival of the arts very much: the habit of discriminating between right and wrong, the sense of pleasure in drawing a good line, would really, I think, be education in the due sense of the word for all such people as had the germs of invention in them ; yet as aforesaid, in this age of the world it would be mere affectation to pretend to shut one's eyes to the art of past ages: that also we must study. If other circumstances, social and economical, do not stand in our way, that is to say, if the world is not too busy to allow us to have Decorative Arts at all, these two are the *direct* means by which we shall get them ; that is, general

cultivation of the powers of the mind, general cultivation of the powers of the eye and hand.

Perhaps that seems to you very commonplace
advice and a very roundabout road; nevertheless
't is a certain one, if by any road you desire to
come to the new art, which is my subject to-night:
if you do not, and if those germs of invention,
which, as I said just now, are no doubt still common enough among men, are left neglected and
undeveloped, the laws of Nature will assert themselves in this as in other matters, and the faculty
of design itself will gradually fade from the race of
man.   Sirs, shall we approach nearer to perfection
by casting away so large a part of that intelligence
which makes us *men?*

And now before I make an end, I want to call
your attention to certain things, that, owing to our
neglect of the arts for other business, bar that good
road to us and are such an hindrance, that, till they
are dealt with, it is hard even to make a beginning
of our endeavor.   And if my talk should seem to
grow too serious for our subject, as indeed I think
it cannot do, I beg you to remember what I said
earlier, of how the arts all hang together.   Now
there is one art of which the old architect of
Edward the Third's time was thinking — he who
founded New College at Oxford, I mean — when he
took this for his motto: 'Manners maketh man:'
he meant by manners the art of morals, the art of
living worthily, and like a man.   I must needs
claim this art also as dealing with my subject.

There is a great deal of sham work in the world, hurtful to the buyer, more hurtful to the seller, if he only knew it, most hurtful to the maker : how good a foundation it would be toward getting good Decorative Art, that is ornamental workmanship, if we craftsmen were to resolve to turn out nothing but excellent workmanship in all things, instead of having, as we too often have now, a very low average standard of work, which we often fall below.

I do not blame either one class or another in this matter, I blame all : to set aside our own class of handicraftsmen, of whose shortcomings you and I know so much that we need talk no more about it, I know that the public in general are set on having things cheap, being so ignorant that they do not know when they get them nasty also ; so ignorant that they neither know nor care whether they give a man his due : I know that the manufacturers (so called) are so set on carrying out competition to its utmost, competition of cheapness, not of excellence, that they meet the bargain-hunters half way, and cheerfully furnish them with nasty wares at the cheap rate they are asked for, by means of what can be called by no prettier name than fraud. England has of late been too much busied with the counting-house and not enough with the workshop : with the result that the counting-house at the present moment is rather barren of orders.

I say all classes are to blame in this matter, but also I say that the remedy lies with the handicraftsmen, who are not ignorant of these things like the public, and who have no call to be greedy and isolated like the manufacturers or middlemen ; the duty and honor of educating the public lies with them, and they have in them the seeds of order and organization which make that duty the easier.

When will they see to this and help to make men of us all by insisting on this most weighty piece of manners ; so that we may adorn life with the pleasure of cheerfully *buying* goods at their due price ; with the pleasure of *selling* goods that we could be proud of both for fair price and fair workmanship : with the pleasure of working soundly and without haste at *making* goods that we could be proud of ? — much the greatest pleasure of the three is that last, such a pleasure as, I think, the world has none like it.

You must not say that this piece of manners lies out of my subject : it is essentially a part of it and most important : for I am bidding you learn to be artists, if art is not to come to an end amongst us : and what is an artist but a workman who is determined that, whatever else happens, his work shall be excellent ? or, to put it in another way : the decoration of workmanship, what is it but the expression of man's pleasure in successful labor ? But what pleasure can there be in *bad* work, in *un*successful labor ; why should we decorate *that?* and how can we bear to be always unsuccessful in our labor ?

As greed of unfair gain, wanting to be paid for what we have not earned, cumbers our path with this tangle of bad work, of sham work, so the heaped-up money which this greed has brought us (for greed will have its way, like all other strong passions), this money, I say, gathered into heaps little and big, with all the false distinction which so unhappily it yet commands amongst us, has raised up against the arts a barrier of the love of luxury and show, which is of all obvious hindrances the worst to overpass : the highest and most cultivated classes are not free from the vulgarity of it, the lower are not free from its pretence. I beg you to remember both as a remedy against this, and as explaining exactly what I mean, that nothing can be a work of art which is not useful ; that is to say, which does not minister to the body when well under command of the mind, or which does not amuse, soothe, or elevate the mind in a healthy state. What tons upon tons of unutterable rubbish pretending to be works of art in some degree would this maxim clear out of our London houses, if it were understood and acted upon ! To my mind it is only here and there (out of the kitchen) that you can find in a well-to-do house things that are of any use at all : as a rule all the decoration (so called) that has got there is there, for the sake of show, not because anybody likes it. I repeat, this stupidity goes through all classes of society : the silk curtains in my Lord's drawing-room are no

more a matter of art to him than the powder in his
footman's hair; the kitchen in a country farmhouse
is most commonly a pleasant and homelike place,
the parlor dreary and useless.

Simplicity of life, begetting simplicity of taste,
that is, a love for sweet and lofty things, is of all
matters most necessary for the birth of the new
and better art we crave for; simplicity everywhere,
in the palace as well as in the cottage.

Still more is this necessary, cleanliness and
decency everywhere, in the cottage as well as in
the palace: the lack of that is a serious piece of
manners for us to correct: that lack and all the in-
equalities of life, and the heaped-up thoughtlessness
and disorder of so many centuries that cause it: and
as yet it is only a very few men who have begun to
think about a remedy for it in its widest range:
even in its narrower aspect, in the defacements of
our big towns by all that commerce brings with it,
who heeds it? who tries to control their squalor
and hideousness? there is nothing but thoughtlessness and recklessness in the matter: the helpless-
ness of people who don't live long enough to do a
thing themselves, and have not manliness and foresight enough to begin the work, and pass it on to
those that shall come after them.

Is money to be gathered? Cut down the pleasant trees among the houses, pull down ancient and
venerable buildings for the money that a few square
yards of London dirt will fetch; blacken rivers,

hide the sun and poison the air with smoke and worse, and it's nobody's business to see to it or mend it: that is all that modern commerce, the counting-house forgetful of the workshop, will do for us herein.

And Science — we have loved her well, and followed her diligently, what will she do? I fear she is so much in the pay of the counting-house, the counting-house and the drill-sergeant, that she is too busy, and will for the present do nothing. Yet there are matters which I should have thought easy for her; say, for example, teaching Manchester how to consume its own smoke, or Leeds how to get rid of its superfluous black dye without turning it into the river, which would be as much worth her attention as the production of the heaviest of heavy black silks, or the biggest of useless guns. Anyhow, however it be done, unless people care about carrying on their business without making the world hideous, how can they care about art? I know it will cost much both of time and money to better these things even a little; but I do not see how these can be better spent than in making life cheerful and honorable for others and for ourselves; and the gain of good life to the country at large that would result from men seriously setting about the bettering of the decency of our big towns would be priceless, even if nothing specially good befell the arts in consequence: I do not know that it would; but I should begin to think matters hopeful if men turned their attention to such things, and I repeat, that unless they do so, we can scarcely even begin with any hope our endeavors for the bettering of the Arts.

Until something or other is done to give all men some pleasure for the eyes and rest for the mind in the aspect of their own and their neighbors' houses, until the contrast is less disgraceful between the fields where beasts live and the streets where men live, I suppose that the practice of the arts must be mainly kept in the hands of a few highly cultivated men, who can go often to beautiful places, whose education enables them, in the contemplation of the past glories of the world, to shut out from their view the every-day squalors that the most of men move in.   Sirs, I believe that art has such sympathy with cheerful freedom, openheartedness and reality, so much she sickens under selfishness and luxury, that she will not live thus isolated and exclusive.   I will go further than this, and say that on such terms I do not wish her to live.   I protest that it would be a shame to an honest artist to enjoy what he had huddled up to himself of such art, as it would be for a rich man to sit and eat dainty food amongst starving soldiers in a beleaguered fort.

I do not want art for a few, any more than education for a few, or freedom for a few.

No, rather than art should live this poor thin life among a few exceptional men, despising those beneath them for an ignorance for which they themselves are responsible, for a brutality that they will not struggle with, — rather than this, I would that the world should indeed sweep away all art for awhile, as I said before I thought it possible she might do: rather than the wheat should rot in the miser's granary, I would that the earth had it, that it might yet have a chance to quicken in the dark.

I have a sort of faith, though, that this clearing away of all art will not happen, that men will get wiser, as well as more learned; that many of the intricacies of life, on which we now pride ourselves more than enough, partly because they are new, partly because they have come with the gain of better things, will be cast aside as having played their part, and being useful no longer. I hope that we shall have leisure from war, — war commercial, as well as war of the bullet and the bayonet; leisure from the knowledge that darkens counsel; leisure above all from the greed of money, and the craving for that overwhelming distinction that money now brings: I believe that as we have even now partly achieved LIBERTY, so we shall one day achieve EQUALITY, which, and which only, means FRATERNITY, and so have leisure from poverty and all its griping, sordid cares.

Then, having leisure from all these things, amidst renewed simplicity of life we shall have leisure to think about our work, that faithful daily companion, which no man any longer will venture to call the Curse of labor: for surely then we shall be happy in it, each in his place, no man grudging at another; no one bidden to be any man's *servant,* every one scorning to be any man's *master:* men will then assuredly be happy in their work, and that happiness will assuredly bring forth decorative, noble, *popular* art.

That art will make our streets as beautiful as the woods, as elevating as the mountain-sides: it' will be a pleasure and a rest, and not a weight upon the spirits to come from the open country into a town; every man's house will be fair and decent, soothing to his mind and helpful to his work: all the works of man that we live amongst and handle will be in harmony with nature, will be reasonable and beautiful: yet all will be simple and inspiriting, not childish nor enervating; for as nothing of beauty and splendor that man's mind and hand may compass shall be wanted from our public buildings, so in no private dwelling will there be any signs of waste, pomp, or insolence, and every man will have his share of the *best.*

It is a dream, you may say, of what has never been and never will be: true, it has never been, and therefore, since the world is alive and moving yet, my hope is the greater that it one day will be: true, it is a dream; but dreams have before now come about of things so good and necessary to us, that we scarcely think of them more than of the daylight, though once people had to live without them, without even the hope of them.

Anyhow, dream as it is, I pray you to pardon my setting it before you, for it lies at the bottom of all my work in the Decorative Arts, nor will it ever be out of my thoughts : and I am here with you to-night to ask you to help me in realizing this dream, this *hope*.

THE ART OF THE PEOPLE.

'And the men of labor spent their strength in daily struggling for breath to maintain the vital strength they labored with: so living in a daily circulation of sorrow, living but to work, and working but to live, as if daily bread were the only end of a wearisome life, and a wearisome life the only occasion of daily bread.' — DANIEL DEFOE.

I KNOW that a large proportion of those here present are either already practising the Fine Arts, or are being specially educated to that end, and I feel that I may be expected to address myself specially to these. But since it is not to be doubted that we are *all* met together because of the interest we take in what concerns these Arts, I would rather address myself to you *all* as representing the public in general. Indeed, those of you who are specially studying Art could learn little of me that would be useful to yourselves only. You are already learning under competent masters — most competent, I am glad to know — by means of a system which should teach you all you need, if you have been right in making the first step of devoting yourselves to Art; I mean if you are aiming at the right thing, and in some way or another understand what Art means, which you may well do without being able to express it, and if you are resolute to follow on the path which that inborn knowledge has shown to you; if it is otherwise with you than this, no system and no teachers will help you to produce real art of any kind, be it never so humble. Those of you who are real artists know well enough all the special advice I can give you, and in how few words it may be said — follow nature, study antiquity, make your own art, and do not steal it, grudge no expense of trouble, patience, or courage, in the striving to accomplish the hard thing you have set yourselves to do. You have had all that said to you twenty times, I doubt not; and twenty times twenty have said it to yourselves, and now I have said it again to you, and done neither you nor me good nor harm thereby. So true it all is, so well known, and so hard to follow.

But to me, and I hope to you, art is a very serious thing, and cannot by any means be dissociated from the weighty matters that occupy the thoughts of men ; and there are principles underlying the practice of .it, on which all serious-minded men may — nay, must — have their own thoughts. It is on some of these that I ask your leave to speak, and to address myself, not only to those who are consciously interested in the arts, but to all those also who have considered what the progress of civilization promises and threatens to those who shall come after us : what there is to hope and fear for the future of the arts, which were born with the

birth of civilization and will only die with its death
— what on this side of things, the present time of
strife and doubt and change, is preparing for the
better time, when the change shall have come, the
strife be lulled, and the doubt cleared : this is a
question, I say, which is indeed weighty, and may
well interest all thinking men.

Nay, so universally important is it, that I fear
lest you should think I am taking too much upon
myself to speak to you on so weighty a matter, nor
should I have dared to do so, if I did not feel that
I am to-night only the mouthpiece of better men
than myself, whose hopes and fears I share ; and
that being so, I am the more emboldened to speak
out, if I can, my full mind on the subject, because
I am in a city where, if anywhere, men are not
contented to live wholly for themselves and the
present, but have fully accepted the duty of keeping
their eyes open to whatever new is stirring, so that
they may help and be helped by any truth that
there may be in it. Nor can I forget, that, since
you have done me the great honor of choosing me
for the President of your Society of Arts for the
past year, and of asking me to speak to you to-
night, I should be doing less than my duty if I did
not, according to my lights, speak out straightfor-
wardly whatever seemed to me might be in a small
degree useful to you. Indeed, I think I am among
friends, who may forgive me if I speak rashly, but
scarcely if I speak falsely.

The aim of your Society and School of Arts is, as I understand it, to further those arts by education widely spread. A very great object is that, and well worthy of the reputation of this great city ; but since Birmingham has also, I rejoice to know, a great reputation for not allowing things to go about shamming life when the brains are knocked out of them, I think you should know and see clearly what it is you have undertaken to further by these institutions, and whether you really care about it, or only languidly acquiesce in it — whether, in short, you know it to the heart, and are indeed part and parcel of it, with your own will, or against it ; or else have heard say that it is a good thing if any one care to meddle with it.

If you are surprised at my putting that question for your consideration, I will tell you why I do so. There are some of us who love Art most, and I may say most faithfully, who see for certain that such love is rare now-a-days. We cannot help seeing, that besides a vast number of people, who (poor souls !) are sordid and brutal of mind and habits, and have had no chance or choice in the matter, there are many high-minded, thoughtful, and cultivated men who inwardly think the arts to be a foolish accident of civilization — nay worse perhaps, a nuisance, a disease, a hindrance to human progress. Some of these, doubtless, are very busy about other sides of thought. They are, as I should put it, so *artistically* engrossed by the

study of science, politics, or what not, that they
have necessarily narrowed their minds by their
hard and praiseworthy labors.   But since such
men are few, this does not account for a prevalent
habit of thought that looks upon Art as at best
trifling.

What is wrong, then, with us or the arts, since
what was once accounted so glorious, is now deemed
paltry?

The question is no light one; for, to put the
matter in its clearest light, I will say that the
leaders of modern thought do for the most part
sincerely and single-mindedly hate and despise the
arts; and you know well that as the leaders are,
so must the people be; and that means that we
who are met together here for the furthering of
Art by wide-spread education are either deceiving
ourselves and wasting our time, since we shall one
day be of the same opinion as the best men among
us, or else we represent a small minority that is
right, as minorities sometimes are, while those
upright men aforesaid, and the great mass of
civilized men, have been blinded by untoward circumstances.

That we are of this mind — the minority that
is right — is, I hope, the case. I hope we know
assuredly that the arts we have met together to
further are necessary to the life of man, if the progress of civilization is not to be as causeless as the
turning of a wheel that makes nothing.

How, then, shall we, the minority, carry out the duty which our position thrusts upon us of striving to grow into a majority?

If we could only explain to those thoughtful men, and the millions of whom they are the flower, what the thing is that we love, which is to us as the bread we eat, and the air we breathe, but about which they know nothing and feel nothing, save a vague instinct of repulsion, then the seed of victory might be sown. This is hard indeed to do; yet if we ponder upon a chapter of ancient or mediæval history, it seems to me some glimmer of a chance of doing so breaks in upon us. Take, for example, a century of the Byzantine Empire, weary yourselves with reading the names of the pedants, tyrants, and tax-gatherers to whom the terrible chain which long-dead Rome once forged, still gave the power of cheating people into thinking that they were necessary lords of the world. Turn then to the lands they governed, and read and forget a long string of the causeless murders of Northern and Saracen pirates and robbers. That is pretty much the sum of what so-called history has left us of the tale of those days — the stupid languor and the evil deeds of kings and scoundrels. Must we turn away then, and say that all was evil. How then did men live from day to day? How then did Europe grow into intelligence and freedom? It seems there were others than those of whom history (so called) has left us the names and the

deeds.   These, the raw material for the treasury
and the slave-market, we now call ' the people,' and
we know that they were working all that while.
Yes, and that their work was not merely slaves'
work, the meal-trough before them and the whip
behind them ; for though history (so called) has forgotten them, yet their work has not been forgotten,
but has made another history — the history of Art.
There is not an ancient city in the East or the
West that does not bear some token of their grief,
and joy, and hope.   From Ispahan to Northumber-
land, there is no building built between the seventh
and seventeenth centuries that does not show the
influence of the labor of that oppressed and
neglected herd of men.   No one of them, indeed,
rose high above his fellows.   There was no Plato,
or Shakespeare, or Michael Angelo amongst them.
Yet, scattered as it was among many men, how
strong their thought was, how long it abided, how
far it travelled !

And so it was ever through all those days
when Art was vigorous and progressive.   Who
can say how little we should know of many periods,
but for their art ?   History (so called) has remembered the kings and warriors, because they destroyed ; Art has remembered the people, because
they created.

I think, then, that this knowledge we have of
the life of past times gives us some token of the
way we should take in meeting those honest and

single-hearted men who above all things desire the world's progress, but whose minds are, as it were, sick on this point of the arts. Surely we may say to them : When all is gained that you (and we) so long for, what shall we do then ? That great change which we are working for, each in his own way, will come like other changes, as a thief in the night, and will be with us before we know it ; but let us imagine that its consummation has come suddenly and dramatically, acknowledged and hailed by all right-minded people ; and what shall we do then, lest we begin once more to heap up fresh corruption for the woeful labor of ages once again ? I say, as we turn away from the flagstaff where the new banner has been just run up ; as we depart, our ears yet ringing with the blare of the heralds' trumpets that have proclaimed the new order of things, what shall we turn to then, what *must* we turn to then ?

To what else, save to our work, our daily labor ?

With what, then, shall we adorn it when we have become wholly free and reasonable ? It is necessary toil, but shall it be toil only ? Shall all we can do with it be to shorten the hours of that toil to the utmost, that the hours of leisure may be long beyond what men used to hope for ? and what then shall we do with the leisure, if we say that all toil is irksome ? Shall we sleep it all away ? — Yes, and never wake again, I should hope, in that case.

What shall we do then ? what shall our necessary hours of labor bring forth ?

That will be a question for all men in that day when many wrongs are righted, and when there will be no classes of degradation on whom the dirty work of the world can be shovelled ; and if men's minds are still sick and loathe the arts, they will not be able to answer that question.

Once men sat under grinding tyrannies, amidst violence and fear so great, that now-a-days we wonder how they lived through twenty-four hours of it, till we remember that then, as now, their daily labor was the main part of their lives, and that that daily labor was sweetened by the daily creation of Art; and shall we, who are delivered from the evils they bore, live drearier days than they did ? Shall men, who have come forth from so many tyrannies, bind themselves to yet another one, and become the slaves of nature, piling day upon day of hopeless, useless toil ?   Must this go on worsening till it comes to this at last — that the world shall have come into its inheritance, and with all foes conquered and nought to bind it, shall choose to sit down and labor for ever amidst grim ugliness ? How, then, were all our hopes cheated, what a gulf of despair should we tumble into then ?

In truth, it cannot be ; yet if that sickness of repulsion to the arts were to go on hopelessly, nought else would be, and the extinction of the love of beauty and imagination would prove to be the extinction of civilization. But that sickness the world will one day throw off, yet will, I believe, pass through many pains in so doing, some of which will look very like the death-throes of art, and some, perhaps, will be grievous enough to the poor people of the world; since hard necessity, I doubt, works many of the world's changes, rather than the purblind striving to see, which we call the foresight of man.

Meanwhile, remember that I asked just now, what was amiss in art or in ourselves that this sickness was upon us. Nothing is wrong or can be with art in the abstract — that must always be good for mankind, or we are all wrong together: but with art, as we of these latter days have known it, there is much wrong; nay, what are we here for to-night if that is not so? were not the schools of art founded all over the country some thirty years ago because we had found out that popular art was fading — or perhaps had faded out from amongst us?

As to the progress made since then in this country — and in this country only, if at all — it is hard for me to speak without being either ungracious or insincere, and yet speak I must. I say, then, that an apparent external progress in some ways is obvious, but I do not know how far that is hopeful, for time must try it, and prove whether it be a passing fashion or the first token of a real stir among the great mass of civilized men. To speak

quite frankly, and as one friend to another, I must
needs say that even as I say those words they
seem too good to be true.   And yet — who knows?
— so wont are we to frame history for the future as
well as for the past, so often are our eyes blind
both when we look backward and when we look
forward, because we have been gazing so intently
at our own days, our own lives.   May all be better
than I think it!

At any rate let us count our gains, and set them
against less hopeful signs of the times.   In England, then — and as far as I know, in England only
— painters of pictures have grown, I believe, more
numerous, and certainly more conscientious in their
work, and in some cases — and this more especially
in England — have developed and expressed a sense
of beauty which the world has not seen for the last
three hundred years.   This is certainly a very great
gain, which it is not easy to over-estimate, both for
those who make the pictures and those who use
them.

Furthermore, in England, and in England only,
there has been a great improvement in architecture
and the arts that attend it — arts which it was the
special province of the afore-mentioned schools to
revive and foster.   This, also, is a considerable
gain to the users of the works so made, but I fear
a gain less important to most of those concerned in
making them.

Against these gains we must, I am very sorry

to say, set the fact not easy to be accounted for, that the rest of the civilized world (so called) seems to have done little more than stand still in these matters; and that among ourselves these improvements have concerned comparatively few people, the mass of our population not being in the least touched by them; so that the great bulk of our architecture — the art which most depends on the taste of the people at large — grows worse and worse every day.

I must speak also of another piece of discouragement before I go further. I dare say many of you will remember how emphatically those who first had to do with the movement of which the foundation of our art-schools was a part, called the attention of our pattern-designers to the beautiful works of the East. This was surely most well judged of them, for they bade us look at an art at once beautiful, orderly, living in our own day, and, above all, popular. Now, it is a grievous result of the sickness of civilization that this art is fast disappearing before the advance of western conquest and commerce — fast, and every day faster. While we are met here in Birmingham to further the spread of education in art, Englishmen in India are, in their short-sightedness, actively destroying the very sources of that education — jewelry, metal-work, pottery, calico-printing, brocade-weaving, carpet-making — all the famous and historical arts of the great peninsula have been for long treated as

matters of no importance, to be thrust aside for
the advantage of any paltry scrap of so-called
commerce ; and matters are now speedily coming
to an end there.   I dare say some of you saw the
presents which the native Princes gave to the
Prince of Wales on the occasion of his progress
through India.   I did myself, I will not say with
great disappointment, for I guessed what they would
be like, but with great grief, since there was scarce
here and there a piece of goods among these costly
gifts, things given as great treasures, which faintly
upheld the ancient fame of the cradle of the industrial arts.   Nay, in some cases, it would have
been laughable, if it had not been so sad, to see the
piteous simplicity with which the conquered race
had copied the blank vulgarity of their lords.   And
this deterioration we are now, as I have said,
actively engaged in forwarding.   I have read a
little book,* a handbook to the Indian Court of
last year's Paris Exhibition, which takes the occasion of noting the state of manufactures in India
one by one.   'Art manufactures,' you would call
them ; but, indeed, all manufactures are, or were,
'art manufactures' in India.   Dr. Birdwood, the
author of this book, is of great experience in Indian
life, a man of science, and a lover of the arts.   His
story, by no means a new one to me, or others
interested in the East and its labor, is a sad one

* Now incorporated in the *Handbook of Indian Art*, by Dr.
Birdwood, published by the Science and Art Department.

indeed. The conquered races in their hopelessness are everywhere giving up the genuine practice of their own arts, which we know ourselves, as we have indeed loudly proclaimed, are founded on the truest and most natural principles. The often-praised perfection of these arts is the blossom of many ages of labor and change ; but the conquered races are casting it aside as a thing of no value, so that they may conform themselves to the inferior art, or rather the lack of art, of their conquerors. In some parts of the country the genuine arts are quite destroyed ; in many others nearly so ; in all they have more or less begun to sicken. So much so is this the case, that now for some time the Government has been furthering this deterioration. As for example, no doubt with the best intentions, and certainly in full sympathy with the general English public, both at home and in India, the Government is now manufacturing cheap Indian carpets in the Indian gaols. I do not say that it is a bad thing to turn out real work, or works of art, in gaols ; on the contrary, I think it good if it be properly managed. But in this case, the Government, being, as I said, in full sympathy with the English public, has determined that it will make its wares cheap, whether it make them nasty or not. Cheap and nasty they are, I assure you ; but, though they are the worst of their kind, they would not be made thus, if everything did not tend the same way. And it is the same everywhere and with all Indian manufactures, till it has come to this — that these poor people have all but lost the one distinction, the one glory that conquest had left them.　Their famous wares, so praised by those who thirty years ago began to attempt the restoration of popular art amongst ourselves, are no longer to be bought at reasonable prices in the common market, but must be sought for and treasured as precious relics for the museums we have founded for our art education.　In short, their art is dead, and the commerce of modern civilization has slain it.

What is going on in India is also going on, more or less, all over the East ; but I have spoken of India chiefly because I cannot help thinking that we ourselves are responsible for what is happening there.　Chance-hap has made us the lords of many millions out there ; surely, it behoves us to look to it, lest we give to the people whom we have made helpless, scorpions for fish and stones for bread.

But since neither on this side, nor on any other, can art be amended, until the countries that lead civilization are themselves in a healthy state about it, let us return to the consideration of its condition among ourselves.　And again I say, that obvious as is that surface improvement of the arts within the last few years, I fear too much that there is something wrong about the root of the plant to exult over the bursting of its February buds.

I have just shown you for one thing that lovers

of Indian and Eastern Art, including as they do the
heads of our institutions for art education, and I am
sure many among what are called the governing
classes, are utterly powerless to stay its downward
course.   The general tendency of civilization is
against them, and is too strong for them.

Again, though many of us love architecture
dearly, and believe that it helps the healthiness
both of body and soul to live among beautiful things,
we of the big towns are mostly compelled to live
in houses which have become a by-word of contempt for their ugliness and inconvenience.   The
stream of civilization is against us, and we cannot
battle against it.

Once more those devoted men who have upheld
the standard of truth and beauty amongst us, and
whose pictures, painted amidst difficulties that none
but a painter can know, show qualities of mind
unsurpassed in any age — these great men have
but a narrow circle that can understand their works,
and are utterly unknown to the great mass of the
people : civilization is so much against them, that
they cannot move the people.

Therefore, looking at all this, I cannot think that
all is well with the root of the tree we are culti-
vating.   Indeed, I believe that if other things were
but to stand still in the world, this improvement
before mentioned would lead to a kind of art which,
in that impossible case, would be in a way stable,
would perhaps stand still also.   This would be an

art cultivated professedly by a few, and for a few, who would consider it necessary — a duty, if they could admit duties — to despise the common herd, to hold themselves aloof from all that the world has been struggling for from the first, to guard carefully every approach to their palace of art. It would be a pity to waste many words on the prospect of such a school of art as this, which does in a way, theoretically at least, exist at present, and has for its watchword a piece of slang that does not mean the harmless thing it seems to mean — art for art's sake. Its fore-doomed end must be, that art at last will seem too delicate a thing for even the hands of the initiated to touch ; and the initiated must at last sit still and do nothing — to the grief of no one.

Well, certainly, if I thought you were come here to further such an art as this I could not have stood up and called you *friends ;* though such a feeble folk as I have told you of one could scarce care to call foes.

Yet, as I say, such men exist, and I have troubled you with speaking of them, because I know that those honest and intelligent people, who are eager for human progress, and yet lack part of the human senses, and are anti-artistic, suppose that such men are artists, and that this is what art means, and what it does for people, and that such a narrow, cowardly life is what we, fellow-handicraftsmen, aim at. I see this taken for granted continually, even by many who, to say truth, ought to know better, and I long to put the slur from off us; to make people understand that we, least of all men, wish to widen the gulf between the classes, nay, worse still, to make new classes of elevation, and new classes of degradation — new lords and new slaves; that we, least of all men, want to cultivate the 'plant called man' in different ways — here stingily, there wastefully : I wish people to understand that the art we are striving for is a good thing that all can share, that will elevate all; in good sooth, if all people do not soon share it there will soon be none to share; if all are not elevated by it, mankind will lose the elevation it has gained. Nor is such an art as we long for a vain dream; such an art once was in times that were worse than these; when there was less courage, kindness, and truth in the world than there is now; such an art there will be hereafter, when there will be more courage, kindness, and truth than there is now in the world.

Let us look backward in history once more for a short while, and then steadily forward till my words are done : I began by saying that part of the common and necessary advice given to Art students was to study antiquity ; and no doubt many of you, like me, have done so; have wandered, for instance, through the galleries of the admirable museum of South Kensington, and, like me, have been filled with wonder and gratitude

at the beauty which has been born from the brain
of man.   Now, consider, I pray you, what these
wonderful works are, and how they were made;
and indeed, it is neither in extravagance nor without due meaning that I use the word 'wonderful'
in speaking of them.   Well, these things are just
the common household goods of those past days,
and that is one reason why they are so few and so
carefully treasured.   They were common things
in their own day, used without fear of breaking or
spoiling — no rarities then — and yet we have called
them 'wonderful.'

And how were they made?   Did a great artist
draw the designs for them — a man of cultivation,
highly paid, daintily fed, carefully housed, wrapped
up in cotton wool, in short, when he was not at
work?   By no means.   Wonderful as these works
are, they were made by 'common fellows,' as the
phrase goes, in the common course of their daily
labor.   Such were the men we honor in honoring
those works.   And their labor — do you think it
was irksome to them?   Those of you who are
artists know very well that it was not; that it could
not be.   Many a grin of pleasure, I'll be bound —
and you will not contradict me — went to the carrying through of those mazes of mysterious beauty, to
the invention of those strange beasts and birds and
flowers that we ourselves have chuckled over at
South Kensington.   While they were at work, at
least, these men were not unhappy, and I suppose

they worked most days, and the most part of the day, as we do.

Or those treasures of architecture that we study so carefully now-a-days — what are they? how were they made? There are great minsters among them, indeed, and palaces of kings and lords, but not many; and, noble and awe-inspiring as these may be, they differ only in size from the little gray church that still so often makes the commonplace English landscape beautiful, and the little gray house that still, in some parts of the country at least, makes an English village a thing apart, to be seen and pondered on by all who love romance and beauty. These form the mass of our architectural treasures, the houses that every-day people lived in, the unregarded churches in which they worshipped.

And, once more, who was it that designed and ornamented them? The great architect, carefully kept for the purpose, and guarded from the common troubles of common men? By no means. Sometimes, perhaps, it was the monk, the ploughman's brother; oftenest his other brother, the village carpenter, smith, mason, what not — 'a common fellow,' whose common, every-day labor fashioned works that are to-day the wonder and despair of many a hard-working 'cultivated' architect. And did he loathe his work? No, it is impossible. I have seen, as we most of us have, work done by such men in some out-of-the-way hamlet — where to-day even few strangers ever come, and

whose people seldom go five miles from their own
doors ; in such places, I say, I have seen work so
delicate, so careful, and so inventive, that nothing in
its way could go further.   And I will assert, without fear of contradiction, that no human ingenuity
can produce work such as this without pleasure
being a third party to the brain that conceived and
the hand that fashioned it.   Nor are such works
rare.   The throne of the great Plantagenet, or the
great Valois, was no more daintily carved than the
seat of the village mass-john, or the chest of the yeoman's good-wife.

So, you see, there was much going on to make
life endurable in those times.   Not every day, you
may be sure, was a day of slaughter and tumult,
though the histories read almost as if it were so ;
but every day the hammer chinked on the anvil,
and the chisel played about the oak beam, and
never without some beauty and invention being born
of it, and consequently some human happiness.

That last word brings me to the very kernel and
heart of what I have come here to say to you, and I
pray you to think of it most seriously — not as to my
words, but as to a thought which is stirring in the
world, and will one day grow into something.

That thing which I understand by real art is the
expression by man of his pleasure in labor.   I do
not believe he can be happy in his labor without
expressing that happiness ; and especially is this so
when he is at work at anything in which he specially

excels.   A most kind gift is this of nature, since all
men, nay, it seems all things too, must labor ; so
that not only does the dog take pleasure in hunting,
and the horse in running, and the bird in flying, but
so natural does the idea seem to us, that we imagine
to ourselves that the earth and the very elements
rejoice in doing their appointed work ; and the
poets have told us of the spring meadows smiling,
of the exultation of the fire, of the countless laughter
of the sea.

Nor until these latter days has man ever rejected
this universal gift, but always, when he has not been
too much perplexed, too much bound by disease or
beaten down by trouble, has striven to make his
work at least, happy.   Pain he has too often found
in his pleasure, and weariness in his rest, to trust to
these.   What matter if his happiness lie with what
must be always with him — his work ?

And, once more, shall we, who have gained so
much, forego this gain, the earliest, most natural
gain of mankind ?   If we have to a great extent
done so, as I verily fear we have, what strange fog-
lights must have misled us ; or rather let me say,
how hard pressed we must have been in the battle
with the evils we have overcome, to have forgotten
the greatest of all evils.   I cannot call it less than
that.   If a man has work to do which he despises,
which does not satisfy his natural and rightful desire
for pleasure, the greater part of his life must pass
unhappily and without self-respect.   Consider, I

beg of you, what that means, and what ruin must
come of it in the end.

If I could only persuade you of this, that the
chief duty of the civilized world to-day, is to set
about making labor happy for all, to do its utmost
to minimize the amount of unhappy labor — nay, if
I could only persuade some two or three of you
here present — I should have made a good night's
work of it.

Do not, at any rate, shelter yourselves from any
misgiving you may have behind the fallacy that the
art-lacking labor of to-day is happy work : for the
most of men it is not so.   It would take long,
perhaps, to show you, and make you fully understand that the would-be art which it produces is
joyless.   But there is another token of its being
most unhappy work, which you cannot fail to understand at once — a grievous thing that token is —
and I beg of you to believe that I feel the full
shame of it, as I stand here speaking of it ; but if
we do not admit that we are sick, how can we be
healed ?   This hapless token is, that the work done
by the civilized world is mostly dishonest work.
Look now : I admit that civilization does make certain things well, things which it knows, consciously
or unconsciously, are necessary to its present unhealthy condition.   These things, to speak shortly,
are chiefly machines for carrying on the competition
in buying and selling, called falsely commerce ; and
machines for the violent destruction of life — that is

to say, materials for two kinds of war; of which kinds the last is no doubt the worst, not so much in itself perhaps, but, because on this point the conscience of the world is beginning to be somewhat pricked. But on the other hand, matters for the carrying on of a dignified daily life, that life of mutual trust, forbearance, and help, which is the only real life of thinking men — these things the civilized world makes ill, and even increasingly worse and worse.

If I am wrong in saying this, you know well I am only saying what is widely thought, nay widely said too, for that matter. Let me give an instance, familiar enough, of that wide-spread opinion. There is a very clever book of pictures * now being sold at the railway bookstalls, called 'The British Working Man, by one who does not believe in him,' — a title and a book which make me both angry and ashamed, because the two express much injustice, and not a little truth in their quaint, and necessarily exaggerated way. It is quite true, and very sad to say, that if any one now-a-days wants a piece of ordinary work done by gardener, carpenter, mason, dyer, weaver, smith, what you will, he will be a lucky rarity if he get it well done. He will, on the contrary, meet on every side with evasion of plain duties, and disregard of other men's rights; yet I cannot see how the 'British Working Man' is to be made to bear the whole burden of this blame, or

* These were originally published in *Fun*.

indeed the chief part of it. I doubt if it be possible
for a whole mass of men to do work to which they
are driven, and in which there is no hope and no
pleasure, without trying to shirk it — at any rate,
shirked it has always been under such circumstances.
On the other hand, I know that there are some men
so right-minded, that they will, in despite of irk-
someness and hopelessness, drive right through their
work.   Such men are the salt of the earth.   But
must there not be something wrong with a state of
society which drives these into that bitter heroism,
and the most part into shirking, into the depths
often of half-conscious self-contempt and degradation?   Be sure that there is, that the blindness and
hurry of civilization, as it now is, have to answer a
heavy charge as to that enormous amount of pleas-
ureless work — work that tries every muscle of the
body and every atom of the brain, and which is
done without pleasure and without aim — work
which everybody who has to do with tries to shuffle
off in the speediest way that dread of starvation or
ruin will allow him.

I am as sure of one thing as that I am living
and breathing, and it is this: that the dishonesty
in the daily arts of life, complaints of which are in
all men's mouths, and which I can answer for it
does exist, is the natural and inevitable result of the
world in the hurry of the war of the counting-house,
and the war of the battlefield, having forgotten — of
all men, I say, each for the other, having forgotten,

that pleasure in our daily labor, which nature cries out for as its due.

Therefore, I say again, it is necessary to the further progress of civilization that men should turn their thoughts to some means of limiting, and in the end of doing away with, degrading labor.

I do not think my words hitherto spoken have given you any occasion to think that I mean by this either hard or rough labor ; I do not pity men much for their hardships, especially if they be accidental ; not necessarily attached to one class or one condition, I mean. Nor do I think (I were crazy or dreaming else) that the work of the world can be carried on without rough labor ; but I have seen enough of that to know that it need not be by any means degrading. To plough the earth, to cast the net, to fold the flock — these, and such as these, which are rough occupations enough, and which carry with them many hardships, are good enough for the best of us, certain conditions of leisure, freedom, and due wages being granted. As to the bricklayer, the mason, and the like — these would be artists, and doing not only necessary, but beautiful, and therefore happy work, if art were anything like what it should be. No, it is not such labor as this which we need to do away with, but the toil which makes the thousand and one things which nobody wants, which are used merely as the counters for the competitive buying and selling, falsely called commerce, which I have

spoken of before — I know in my heart, and not
merely by my reason, that this toil cries out to be
done away with.   But, besides that, the labor
which now makes things good and necessary in
themselves, merely as counters for the commercial
war aforesaid, needs regulating and reforming. Nor
can this reform be brought about save by art ; and
if we were only come to our right minds, and could
see the necessity for making labor sweet to all men,
as it is now to very few — the necessity, I repeat ;
lest discontent, unrest, and despair should at last
swallow up all society — If we, then, with our eyes
cleared, could but make some sacrifice of things
which do us no good, since we unjustly and un-
easily possess them, then indeed I believe we should
sow the seeds of a happiness which the world has
not yet known, of a rest and content which would
make it what I cannot help thinking it was meant
to be: and with that seed would be sown also the
seed of real art, the expression of man's happiness
in his labor, — an art made by the people, and for
the people, as a happiness to the maker and the
user.

That is the only real art there is, the only art
which will be an instrument to the progress of the
world, and not a hindrance. Nor can I seriously
doubt that in your hearts you know that it is so,
all of you, at any rate, who have in you an instinct
for art. I believe that you agree with me in this,
though you may differ from much else that I have

said. I think assuredly that this is the art whose welfare we have met together to further, and the necessary instruction in which we have undertaken to spread as widely as may be.

Thus I have told you something of what I think is to be hoped and feared for the future of art; and if you ask me what I expect as the practical outcome of the admission of these opinions, I must say at once that I know, even if we were all of one mind, and that what I think the right mind on this subject, we should still have much work and many hindrances before us; we should still have need of all the prudence, foresight, and industry of the best among us; and, even so, our path would sometimes seem blind enough. And, to-day, when the opinions which we think right, and which one day will be generally thought so, have to struggle sorely to make themselves noticed at all, it is early days for us to try to see our exact and clearly-mapped road. I suppose you will think it too commonplace of me to say that the general education that makes men think, will one day make them think rightly upon art. Commonplace as it is, I really believe it, and am indeed encouraged by it, when I remember how obviously this age is one of transition from the old to the new, and what a strange confusion, from out of which we shall one day come, our ignorance and half-ignorance is like to make of the exhausted rubbish of the old and the crude rubbish of the new, both of which lie so ready to our hands.

But, if I must say, furthermore, any words that seem like words of practical advice, I think my task is hard, and I fear I shall offend some of you whatever I say; for this is indeed an affair of morality, rather than of what people call art.

However, I cannot forget that, in my mind, it is not possible to dissociate art from morality, politics, and religion. Truth in these great matters of principle is of one, and it is only in formal treatises that it can be split up diversely. I must also ask you to remember how I have already said, that though my mouth alone speaks, it speaks, however feebly and disjointedly, the thoughts of many men better than myself. And further, though when things are tending to the best, we shall still, as aforesaid, need our best men to lead us quite right; yet even now surely, when it is far from that, the least of us can do some yeoman's service to the cause, and live and die not without honor.

So I will say that I believe there are two virtues much needed in modern life, if it is ever to become sweet; and I am quite sure that they are absolutely necessary in the sowing the seed of an *art which is to be made by the people and for the people, as a happiness to the maker and the user.* These virtues are honesty, and simplicity of life. To make my meaning clearer I will name the opposing vice of the second of these — luxury to wit. Also I mean by honesty, the careful and eager giving his due to every man, the determination not to gain by.

any man's loss, which in my experience is not a common virtue.

But note how the practice of either of these virtues will make the other easier to us. For if our wants are few, we shall have but little chance of being driven by our wants into injustice; and if we are fixed in the principle of giving every man his due, how can our self-respect bear that we should give too much to ourselves?

And in art, and in that preparation for it without which no art that is stable or worthy can be, the raising, namely, of those classes which have heretofore been degraded, the practice of these virtues would make a new world of it. For if you are rich, your simplicity of life will both go towards smoothing over the dreadful contrast between waste and want, which is the great horror of civilized countries, and will also give an example and standard of dignified life to those classes which you desire to raise, who, as it is indeed, being like enough to rich people, are given both to envy and to imitate the idleness and waste that the possession of much money produces.

Nay, and apart from the morality of the matter, which I am forced to speak to you of, let me tell you that though simplicity in art may be costly as well as uncostly, at least it is not wasteful, and nothing is more destructive to art than the want of it. I have never been in any rich man's house which would not have looked the better for having a bonfire made outside of it of nine-tenths of all that it held. Indeed, our sacrifice on the side of luxury will, it seems to me, be little or nothing: for, as far as I can make out, what people usually mean by it, is either a gathering of possessions which are sheer vexations to the owner, or a chain of pompous circumstance, which checks and annoys the rich man at every step. Yes, luxury cannot exist without slavery of some kind or other, and its abolition will be blessed like the abolition of other slaveries, by the freeing both of the slaves and of their masters.

Lastly, if, besides attaining to simplicity of life, we attain also to the love of justice, then will all things be ready for the new springtime of the arts. For those of us that are employers of labor, how can we bear to give any man less money than he can decently live on, less leisure than his education and self-respect demand? or those of us who are workmen, how can we bear to fail in the contract we have undertaken, or to make it necessary for a foreman to go up and down spying out our mean tricks and evasions? or we the shopkeepers — can we endure to lie about our wares, that we may shuffle off our losses on to some one else's shoulders? or we the public — how can we bear to pay a price for a piece of goods which will help to trouble one man, to ruin another, and starve a third? Or, still more, I think, how can we bear to use, how can we enjoy something which has been a pain and a grief for the maker to make?

And, now, I think, I have said what I came to say. I confess that there is nothing new in it, but you know the experience of the world is that a thing must be said over and over again before any great number of men can be got to listen to it. Let my words to-night, therefore, pass for one of the necessary times that the thought in them must be spoken out.

For the rest I believe that, however seriously these words may be gainsaid, I have been speaking to an audience in whom any words spoken from a sense of duty and in hearty good-will, as mine have been, will quicken thought and sow some good seed. At any rate it is good for a man who thinks seriously to face his fellows, and speak out whatever really burns in him, so that men may seem less strange to one another, and misunderstanding, the fruitful cause of aimless strife, may be avoided.

But if to any of you I have seemed to speak hopelessly, my words have been lacking in art ; and you must remember that hopelessness would have locked my mouth, not opened it. I am, indeed, hopeful, but can I give a date to the accomplishment of my hope, and say that it will happen in my life or yours ?

But I will at least say, Courage ! for things wonderful, unhoped for, glorious, have happened even in this short while I have been alive.

Yes, surely these times are wonderful and fruitful

of change, which, as it wears and gathers new life even in its wearing, will one day bring better things for the toiling days of men, who with freer hearts and clearer eyes, will once more gain the sense of outward beauty, and rejoice in it.

Meanwhile, if these hours be dark, as, indeed, in many ways they are, at least do not let us sit deedless, like fools and fine gentlemen, thinking the common toil not good enough for us, and beaten by the muddle; but rather let us work like good fellows trying by some dim candle-light to set our workshop ready against to-morrow's daylight — that to-morrow, when the civilized world, no longer greedy, strifeful, and destructive, shall have a new art, a glorious art, made by the people and for the people, as a happiness to the maker and the user.

THE BEAUTY OF LIFE.

'——propter vitam vivendi perdere causas.' — *Juvenal.*

I STAND before you this evening weighted with a
disadvantage that I did not feel last year ; — I have
little fresh to tell you ; I can somewhat enlarge on
what I said then ; here and there I may make bold
to give you a practical suggestion, or I may put
what I have to say in a way that will be clearer to
some of you perhaps; but my message is really
the same as it was when I first had the pleasure of
meeting you.

It is true that if all were going smoothly with
art, or at all events so smoothly that there were
but a few malcontents in the world, you might
listen with some pleasure, and perhaps advantage,
to the talk of an old hand in the craft concerning
ways of work, the snares that beset success, and
the shortest road to it, to a tale of workshop receipts and the like : that would be a pleasant talk
surely between friends and fellow-workmen ; but
it seems to me as if it were not for us as yet ; nay,
maybe we may live long and find no time fit for
such restful talk as the cheerful histories of the
hopes and fears of our workshops : anyhow to-night

I cannot do it, but must once again call the faithful of art to a battle wider and more distracting than that kindly struggle with nature, to which all true craftsmen are born ; which is both the building-up and the wearing-away of their lives.

As I look round on this assemblage, and think of all that it represents, I cannot choose but be moved to the soul by the troubles of the life of civilized man, and the hope that thrusts itself through them ; I cannot refrain from giving you once again the message with which, as it seems, some chance-hap has charged me : that message is, in short, to call on you to face the latest danger which civilization is threatened with, a danger of her own breeding : that men in struggling towards the complete attainment of all the luxuries of life for the strongest portion of their race should deprive their whole race of all the beauty of life : a danger that the strongest and wisest of mankind, in striving to attain to a complete mastery over nature, should destroy her simplest and widest-spread gifts, and thereby enslave simple people to them, and themselves to themselves, and so at last drag the world into a second barbarism more ignoble, and a thousandfold more hopeless, than the first.

Now of you who are listening to me, there are some, I feel sure, who have received this message, and taken it to heart, and are day by day fighting the battle that it calls on you to fight : to you I

can say nothing but that if any word I speak discourage you, I shall heartily wish I had never
spoken at all : but to be shown the enemy, and the
castle we have got to storm, is not to be bidden
to run from him ; nor am I telling you to sit down
deedless in the desert because between you and the
promised land lies many a trouble, and death itself
maybe : the hope before you you know, and nothing
that I can say can take it away from you ; but
friend may with advantage cry out to friend in the
battle that a stroke is coming from this side or that
take my hasty words in that sense, I beg of you.

But I think there will be others of you in whom
vague discontent is stirring : who are oppressed by
the life that surrounds you ; confused and troubled
by that oppression, and not knowing on which side
to seek a remedy, though you are fain to do so :
well, we, who have gone further into those troubles,
believe that we can help you : true we cannot at
once take your trouble from you ; nay, we may at
first rather add to it ; but we can tell you what we
think of the way out of it ; and then amidst the
many things you will have to do to set yourselves
and others fairly on that way, you will many days,
nay most days, forget your trouble in thinking of
the good that lies beyond it, for which you are
working.

But, again, there are others amongst you (and
to speak plainly, I daresay they are the majority),
who are not by any means troubled by doubt of

the road the world is going, nor excited by any
hope of its bettering that road : to them the cause
of civilization is simple and even commonplace :
wonder, hope, and fear no longer hang about it ;
it has become to us like the rising and setting of
the sun ; it cannot err, and we have no call to
meddle with it, either to complain of its course, or
to try to direct it.

There is a ground of reason and wisdom in that
way of looking at the matter : surely the world will
go on its ways, thrust forward by impulses which
we cannot understand or sway : but as it grows in
strength for the journey, its necessary food is the
life and aspirations of *all* of us : and we discontented strugglers with what at times seems the
hurrying blindness of civilization, no less than those
who see nothing but smooth, unvarying progress
in it, are bred of civilization also, and shall be
used up to further it in some way or other, I doubt
not : and it may be of some service to those
who think themselves the only loyal subjects of
progress to hear of our existence, since their not
hearing of it would not make an end of it : it may
set them a thinking not unprofitably to hear of
burdens that they do not help to bear, but which
are nevertheless real and weighty enough to some
of their fellow-men, who are helping, even as they
are, to form the civilization that is to be.

The danger that the present course of civilization
will destroy the beauty of life — these are hard

words, and I wish I could mend them, but I cannot while I speak what I believe to be the truth.

That the beauty of life is a thing of no moment, I suppose few people would venture to assert, and yet most civilized people act as if it were of none, and in so doing are wronging both themselves and those that are to come after them ; for that beauty, which is what is meant by *art,* using the word in its widest sense, is, I contend, no mere accident to human life, which people can take or leave as they choose, but a positive necessity of life, if we are to live as nature meant us to; that is, unless we are content to be less than men.

Now I ask you, as I have been asking myself this long while, what proportion of the population in civilized countries has any share at all in that necessity of life ?

I say that the answer which must be made to that question justifies my fear that modern civiliza-tion is on the road to trample out all the beauty of life, and to make us less than men.

Now if there should be any here who will say : It was always so ; there always was a mass of rough ignorance that knew and cared nothing about art ; I answer first, that if that be the case, then it was always wrong, and we, as soon as we have become conscious of that wrong, are bound to set it right if we can.

But moreover, strange to say, and in spite of all the suffering that the world has wantonly made for itself, and has in all ages so persistently clung to, as if it were a good and holy thing, this wrong of the mass of men being regardless of art was *not* always so.

So much is now known of the periods of art that have left abundant examples of their work behind them, that we can judge of the art of all periods by comparing these with the remains of times of which less has been left us ; and we cannot fail to come to the conclusion that down to very recent days everything that the hand of man touched was more or less beautiful : so that in those days all people who made anything shared in art, as well as all people who used the things so made · that is, *all* people shared in art.

But some people may say : And was that to be wished for ? would not this universal spreading of art stop progress in other matters, hinder the work of the world ? Would it not make us unmanly ? or if not that, would it not be intrusive, and push out other things necessary also for men to study ?

Well, I have claimed a necessary place for art, a natural place, and it would be in the very essence of it, that it would apply its own rules of order and fitness to the general ways of life : it seems to me, therefore, that people who are over-anxious of the outward expression of beauty becoming too great a force among the other forces of life, would, if they had had the making of the external world, have been afraid of making an ear of wheat beautiful, lest it should not have been good to eat.

But indeed there seems no chance of art becoming universal, unless on the terms that it shall have little self-consciousness, and for the most part be done with little effort; so that the rough work of the world would be as little hindered by it, as the work of external nature is by the beauty of all her forms and moods : this was the case in the times that I have been speaking of : of art which was made by conscious effort, the result of the individual striving towards perfect expression of their thoughts by men very specially gifted, there was perhaps no more than there is now, except in very wonderful and short periods; though I believe that even for such men the struggle to produce beauty was not so bitter as it now is. But if there were not more great thinkers than there are now, there was a countless multitude of happy workers whose work did express, and could not choose but express, some original thought, and was consequently both interesting and beautiful : now there is certainly no chance of the more individual art becoming common, and either wearying us by its over-abundance, or by noisy self-assertion preventing highly cultivated men taking their due part in the other work of the world ; it is too difficult to do : it will be always but the blossom of all the half-conscious work below it, the fulfilment of the shortcomings of less complete minds : but it will waste much of its power, and have much less influence on men's minds, unless it be surrounded by abundance of that commoner work, in which all men once shared, and which, I say, will, when art has really awakened, be done so easily and constantly, that it will stand in no man's way to hinder him from doing what he will, good or evil.   And as, on the one hand, I believe that art made by the people and for the people as a joy both to the maker and the user would further progress in other matters rather than hinder it, so also I firmly believe that that higher art produced only by great brains and miraculously gifted hands cannot exist without it: I believe that the present state of things in which it does exist, while popular art is, let us say, asleep or sick, is a transitional state, which must end at last either in utter defeat or utter victory for the arts.

For whereas all works of craftsmanship were once beautiful, unwittingly or not, they are now divided into two kinds, works of art and non-works of art: now nothing made by man's hand can be indifferent ; it must be either beautiful and elevating, or ugly and degrading ; and those things that are without art are so aggressively ; they wound it by their existence, and they are now so much in the majority that the works of art we are obliged to set ourselves to seek for, whereas the other things are the ordinary companions of our every-day life ; so that if those who cultivate art intellectually were inclined never so much to wrap themselves in their special gifts and their high cultivation, and so live happily, apart from other men, and despising them, they could not do so: they are as it were living in an enemy's country; at every turn there is something lying in wait to offend and vex their nicer sense and educated eyes: they must share in the general discomfort—and I am glad of it.

So the matter stands: from the first dawn of history till quite modern times, art, which nature meant to solace all, fulfilled its purpose; all men shared in it; that was what made life romantic, as people call it, in those days; that and not robber-barons and inaccessible kings with their hierarchy of serving-nobles and other such rubbish: but art grew and grew, saw empires sicken and sickened with them; grew hale again, and haler, and grew so great at last, that she seemed in good truth to have conquered everything, and laid the material world under foot. Then came a change at a period of the greatest life and hope in many ways that Europe had known till then: a time of so much and such varied hope that people call it the time of the New Birth: as far as the arts are concerned I deny it that title; rather it seems to me that the great men who lived and glorified the practice of art in those days, were the fruit of the old, not the seed of the new order of things: but a stirring and hopeful time it was, and many things were newborn then which have since brought forth fruit enough: and it is strange and perplexing that from those days forward the lapse of time, which, through plenteous confusion and failure, has on the whole been steadily destroying privilege and exclusiveness in other matters, has delivered up art to be the exclusive privilege of a few, and has taken from the people their birthright; while both wronged and wrongers have been wholly unconscious of what they were doing.

Wholly unconscious — yes, but we are no longer so: there lies the sting of it, and there also the hope.

When the brightness of the so-called Renaissance faded, and it faded very suddenly, a deadly chill fell upon the arts: that New-birth mostly meant looking back to past times, wherein the men of those days thought they saw a perfection of art, which to their minds was different in kind, and not in degree only, from the ruder suggestive art of their own fathers: this perfection they were ambitious to imitate, this alone seemed to be art to them, the rest was childishness: so wonderful was their energy, their success so great, that no doubt to commonplace minds among them, though surely not to the great masters, that perfection seemed to be gained: and, perfection being gained, what are you to do?— you can go no further, you must aim at standing still — which you cannot do.

Art by no means stood still in those latter days of the Renaissance, but took the downward road with terrible swiftness, and tumbled down at the bottom of the hill, where as if bewitched it lay long in great content, believing itself to be the art of Michael Angelo, while it was the art of men whom nobody remembers but those who want to sell their pictures.

Thus it fared with the more individual forms of art. As to the art of the people ; in countries and places where the greater art had flourished most, it went step by step on the downward path with that : in more out-of-the-way places, England for instance, it still felt the influence of the life of its earlier and happier days, and in a way lived on a while ; but its life was so feeble, and, so to say, illogical, that it could not resist any change in external circumstances, still less could it give birth to anything new ; and before this century began, its last flicker had died out. Still, while it was living, in whatever dotage, it did imply something going on in those matters of daily use that we have been thinking of, and doubtless satisfied some cravings for beauty : and when it was dead, for a long time people did not know it, or what had taken its place, crept so to say into its dead body — that pretence of art, to wit, which is done with machines, though sometimes the machines are called men, and doubtless are so out of working hours : nevertheless long before it was quite dead it had fallen so low that the whole subject was usually treated with the utmost contempt by every one who had any pretence of being a sensible man, and in short the

whole civilized world had forgotten that there had
ever been an art *made by the people for the people as
a joy for the maker and the user.*

But now it seems to me that the very sudden-
ness of the change ought to comfort us, to make us
look upon this break in the continuity of the golden
chain as an accident only, that itself cannot last:
for think, how many thousand years it may be since
that primæval man graved with a flint splinter on a
bone the story of the mammoth he had seen, or told
us of the slow uplifting of the heavily-horned heads
of the reindeer that he stalked: think I say of the
space of time from then till the dimming of the
brightness of the Italian Renaissance! whereas
from that time till popular art died unnoticed and
despised among ourselves is just but two hundred
years.

Strange too, that very death is contemporaneous
with new-birth of something at all events; for out
of all despair sprang a new time of hope lighted by
the torch of the French Revolution: and things
that had languished with the languishing of art,
rose afresh and surely heralded its new birth: in
good earnest poetry was born again, and the
English Language, which under the hands of syco-
phantic verse-makers had been reduced to a miserable jargon, whose meaning, if it have a meaning,
cannot be made out without translation, flowed
clear, pure, and simple, along with the music of
Blake and Coleridge: take those names, the earliest

in date among ourselves, as a type of the change that has happened in literature since the time of George II.

With that literature in which romance, that is to say humanity, was re-born, there sprang up also a feeling for the romance of external nature, which is surely strong in us now, joined with a longing to know something real of the lives of those who have gone before us ; of these feelings united you will find the broadest expression in the pages of Walter Scott: it is curious as showing how sometimes one art will lag behind another in a revival, that the man who wrote the exquisite and wholly unfettered naturalism of the Heart of Midlothian, for instance, thought himself continually bound to seem to feel ashamed of, and to excuse himself for, his love of Gothic Architecture : he felt that it was romantic, and he knew that it gave him pleasure, but somehow he had not found out that it was art, having been taught in many ways that nothing could be art that was not done by a named man under academical rules.

I need not perhaps dwell much on what of change has been since : you know well that one of the master-arts, the art of painting, has been revolutionized. I have a genuine difficulty in speaking to you of men who are my own personal friends, nay my masters : still since I cannot quite say nothing of them I must say the plain truth, which is this ; never in the whole history of art did any set

of men come nearer to the feat of making something out of nothing than that little knot of painters
who have raised English art from what it was, when
as a boy I used to go to the Royal Academy Exhibition, to what it is now.

It would be ungracious indeed for me who have
been so much taught by him, that I cannot help
feeling continually as I speak that I am echoing
his words, to leave out the name of John Ruskin
from an account of what has happened since the
tide, as we hope, began to turn in the direction of
art. True it is, that his unequalled style of English
and his wonderful eloquence would, whatever its
subject-matter, have gained him some sort of a
hearing in a time that has not lost its relish for
literature; but surely the influence that he has
exercised over cultivated people must be the result
of that style and that eloquence expressing what
was already stirring in men's minds; he could not
have written what he has done unless people were
in some sort ready for it; any more than those
painters could have begun their crusade against the
dulness and incompetency that was the rule in their
art thirty years ago, unless they had some hope that
they would one day move people to understand
them.

Well, we find that the gains since the turning-
point of the tide are these : that there are some few
artists who have, as it were, caught up the golden
chain dropped two hundred years ago, and that

there are a few highly cultivated people who can understand them; and that beyond these there is a vague feeling abroad among people of the same degree, of discontent at the ignoble ugliness that surrounds them.

That seems to me to mark the advance that we have made since the last of popular art came to an end amongst us, and I do not say, considering where we then were, that it is not a great advance, for it comes to this, that though the battle is still to win, there are those who are ready for the battle.

Indeed it would be a strange shame for this age if it were not so: for as every age of the world has its own troubles to confuse it, and its own follies to cumber it, so has each its own work to do, pointed out to it by unfailing signs of the times; and it is unmanly and stupid for the children of any age to say: We will not set our hands to the work; we did not make the troubles, we will not weary ourselves seeking a remedy for them: so heaping up for their sons a heavier load than they can lift without such struggles as will wound and cripple them sorely. Not thus our fathers served us, who, working late and early, left us at last that seething mass of people so terribly alive and energetic, that we call modern Europe; not thus those served us, who have made for us these present days, so fruitful of change and wondering expectation.

The century that is now beginning to draw to an end, if people were to take to nicknaming centuries,

would be called the Century of Commerce ; and I
do not think I undervalue the work that it has
done: it has broken down many a prejudice and
taught many a lesson that the world has been
hitherto slow to learn : it has made it possible for
many a man to live free, who would in other times
have been a slave, body or soul, or both : if it has
not quite spread peace and justice through the
world, as at the end of its first half we fondly hoped
it would, it has at least stirred up in many fresh
cravings for peace and justice: its work has been
good and plenteous, but much of it was roughly
done, as needs was ; recklessness has commonly
gone with its energy, blindness too often with its
haste: so that perhaps it may be work enough for
the next century to repair the blunders of that
recklessness, to clear away the rubbish which that
hurried work has piled up ; nay even we in the
second half of its last quarter may do something
towards setting its house in order.

You, of this great and famous town, for instance,
which has had so much to do with the Century of
Commerce : your gains are obvious to all men, but
the price you have paid for them is obvious to
many — surely to yourselves most of all : I do not
say that they are not worth the price ; I know that
England and the world could very ill afford to
exchange the Birmingham of to-day for the Birmingham of the year 1700 : but surely if what you
have gained be more than a mockery, you cannot

stop at those gains, or even go on always piling up similar ones. Nothing can make me believe that the present condition of your Black Country yonder is an unchangeable necessity of your life and position: such miseries as this were begun and carried on in pure thoughtlessness, and a hundredth part of the energy that was spent in creating them would get rid of them: I do think if we were not all of us too prone to acquiesce in the base bye-word 'after me the deluge,' it would soon be something more than an idle dream to hope that your pleasant midland hills and fields might begin to become pleasant again in some way or other, even without depopulating them ; or that those once lovely valleys of Yorkshire in the 'heavy woollen district,' with their sweeping hill-sides and noble rivers should not need the stroke of ruin to make them once more delightful abodes of men,- instead of the dog-holes that the Century of Commerce has made them.

Well, people will not take the trouble or spend the money necessary to beginning this sort of re-forms, because they do not feel the evils they live amongst, because they have degraded themselves into something less than men ; they are unmanly because they have ceased to have their due share of art.

For again I say that herein rich people have defrauded themselves as well as the poor : you will see a refined and highly educated man now-a-days, who has been to Italy and Egypt, and where not, who can talk learnedly enough (and fantastically enough sometimes) about art, and who has at his fingers' ends abundant lore concerning the art and literature of past days, sitting down without signs of discomfort in a house, that with all its surroundings is just brutally vulgar and hideous : all his education has not done more for him than that.

The truth is, that in art, and in other things besides, the labored education of a few will not raise even those few above the reach of the evils that beset the ignorance of the great mass of the population : the brutality, of which such a huge stock has been accumulated lower down, will often show without much peeling through the selfish refinement of those who have let it accumulate. The lack of art, or rather the murder of art, that curses our streets from the sordidness of the surroundings of the lower classes, has its exact counterpart in the dulness and vulgarity of those of the middle classes, and the double-distilled dulness, and scarcely less vulgarity of those of the upper classes.

I say this is as it should be ; it is just and fair as far as it goes ; and moreover the rich with their leisure are the more like to move if they feel the pinch themselves.

But how shall they and we, and all of us, move ? What is the remedy ?

What remedy can there be for the blunders of civilization but further civilization ? You do not

by any accident think that we have gone as far in
that direction as it is possible to go, do you?—
even in England, I mean?

When some changes have come to pass, that
perhaps will be speedier than most people think,
doubtless education will both grow in quality and
in quantity; so that it may be, that as the nine-
teenth century is to be called the Century of Commerce, the twentieth may be called the Century of
Education.   But that education does not end when
people leave school is now a mere commonplace;
and how then can you really educate men who lead
the life of machines, who only think for the few hours
during which they are not at work, who in short
spend almost their whole lives in doing work which
is not proper for developing them, body and mind,
in some worthy way?   You cannot educate, you
cannot civilize men, unless you can give them a
share in art.

Yes, and it is hard indeed as things go to give
most men that share; for they do not miss it, or
ask for it, and it is impossible as things are that
they should either miss or ask for it.   Nevertheless
everything has a beginning, and many great things
have had very small ones; and since, as I have
said, these ideas are already abroad in more than
one form, we must not be too much discouraged at
the seemingly boundless weight we have to lift.

After all, we are only bound to play our own
parts, and do our own share of the lifting; and as

in no case that share can be great, so also in all cases it is called for, it is necessary.   Therefore let us work and faint not ; remembering that though it be natural, and therefore excusable, amidst doubtful times to feel doubts of success oppress us at whiles, yet not to crush those doubts, and work as if we had them not, is simple cowardice, which is unforgivable.   No man has any right to say that all has been done for nothing, that all the faithful unwearying strife of those who have gone before us shall lead us nowhither ; that mankind will but go round and round in a circle for ever : no man has a right to say that, and then get up morning after morning to eat his victuals and sleep a-nights, all the while making other people toil to keep his worthless life a-going.

Be sure that some way or other will be found out of the tangle, even when things seem most tangled, and be no less sure that some use will then have come of our work, if it has been faithful, and therefore unsparingly careful and thoughtful.

So once more I say, if in any matters civilization has gone astray, the remedy lies not in standing still, but in more complete civilization.

Now whatever discussion there may be about that often used and often misused word, I believe all who hear me will agree with me in believing from their hearts, and not merely in saying in conventional phrase, that the civilization which does not carry the whole people with it, is doomed to fall, and give place to one which at least aims at doing so.

We talk of the civilization of the ancient peoples, of the classical times : well, civilized they were no doubt, some of their folk at least : an Athenian citizen for instance led a simple, dignified, almost perfect life ; but there were drawbacks to happiness perhaps in the life of his slaves : and the civilization of the ancients was founded on slavery.

Indeed that ancient society did give a model to the world, and showed us for ever what blessings are freedom of life and thought, self-restraint and a generous education : all those blessings the ancient free peoples set forth to the world — and kept them to themselves.

Therefore no tyrant was too base, no pretext too hollow, for enslaving the grandsons of the men of Salamis and Thermopylæ : therefore did the descendants of those stern and self-restrained Romans, who were ready to give up everything, and life as the least of things, to the glory of their commonweal, produce monsters of license and reckless folly. Therefore did a little knot of Galilean peasants overthrow the Roman Empire.

Ancient civilization was chained to slavery and exclusiveness, and it fell ; the barbarism that took its place has delivered us from slavery and grown into modern civilization : and that in its turn has before it the choice of never-ceasing growth, or destruction by that which has in it the seeds of higher growth.

There is an ugly word for a dreadful fact, which I must make bold to use — the residuum: that word, since the time I first saw it used, has had a terrible significance to me, and I have felt from my heart that if this residuum were a necessary part of modern civilization, as some people openly, and many more tacitly, assume that it is, then this civilization carries with it the poison that shall one day destroy it, even as its elder sister did: if civilization is to go no further than this, it had better not have gone so far: if it does not aim at getting rid of this misery and giving some share in the happiness and dignity of life to *all* the people that it has created, and which it spends such un-wearying energy in creating, it is simply an or-ganized injustice, a mere instrument for oppression, so much the worse than that which has gone before it, as its pretensions are higher, its slavery subtler, its mastery harder to overthrow, because supported by such a dense mass of commonplace well-being and comfort.

Surely this cannot be: surely there is a dis-tinct feeling abroad of this injustice: so that if the residuum still clogs all the efforts of modern civilization to rise above mere population-breeding and money-making, the difficulty of dealing with it is the legacy, first of the ages of violence and almost conscious brutal injustice, and next of the ages of thoughtlessness, of hurry and blindness: surely all those who think at all of the future of the world are at work in one way or other in striving to rid it of this shame.

That to my mind is the meaning of what we call National Education, which we have begun, and which is doubtless already bearing its fruits, and will bear greater, when all people are educated, not according to the money which they or their parents possess, but according to the capacity of their minds.

What effect that will have upon the future of the arts, I cannot say, but one would surely think a very great effect ; for it will enable people to see clearly many things which are now as completely hidden from them as if they were blind in body and idiotic in mind : and this, I say, will act not only upon those who most directly feel the evils of ignorance, but also upon those who feel them indirectly, — upon us, the educated : the great wave of rising intelligence, rife with so many natural desires and aspirations, will carry all classes along with it, and force us all to see that many things which we have been used to look upon as necessary and eternal evils are merely the accidental and temporary growths of past stupidity, and can be escaped from by due effort, and the exercise of courage, good-will, and forethought.

And among those evils, I do, and must always, believe will fall that one which last year I told you that I accounted the greatest of all evils, the heaviest of all slaveries ; that evil of the greater part of the

population being engaged for by far the most part
of their lives in work, which at the best cannot
interest them, or develop their best faculties, and
at the worst (and that is the commonest, too), is
mere unmitigated slavish toil, only to be wrung out
of them by the sternest compulsion, a toil which
they shirk all they can — small blame to them.
And this toil degrades them into less than men ;
and they will some day come to know it, and cry
out to be made men again, and art only can do it,
and redeem them from this slavery ; and I say once
more that this is her highest and most glorious end
and aim ; and it is in her struggle to attain to it
that she will most surely purify herself, and quicken
her own aspirations towards perfection.

But we — in the meantime we must not sit
waiting for obvious signs of these later and
glorious days to show themselves on earth, and
in the heavens, but rather turn to at the commonplace, and maybe often dull work of fitting ourselves in detail to take part in them if we should
live to see one of them ; or in doing our best to
make the path smooth for their coming, if we are
to die before they are here.

What, therefore, can we do, to guard traditions
of time past that we may not one day have to
begin anew from the beginning with none to teach
us ? What are we to do, that we may take heed
to, and spread the decencies of life, so that at the
least we may have a field where it will be possible

for art to grow when men begin to long for it ·
what finally can we do, each of us, to cherish some
germ of art, so that it may meet with others, and
spread and grow little by little into the thing that
we need ?

Now I cannot pretend to think that the first of
these duties is a matter of indifference to you, after
my experience of the enthusiastic meeting that I
had the honor of addressing here last autumn on
the subject of the (so-called) restoration of St.
Mark's at Venice; you thought, and most justly
thought, it seems to me, that the subject was of
such moment to art in general, that it was a simple
and obvious thing for men who were anxious on
the matter to address themselves to those who had
the decision of it in their hands; even though the
former were called Englishmen, and the latter
Italians; for you felt that the name of lovers of
art would cover those differences: if you had any
misgivings, you remembered that there was but
one such building in the world, and that it was
worth while risking a breach of etiquette, if any
words of ours could do anything towards saving
it: well, the Italians were, some of them, very
naturally, though surely unreasonably, irritated,
for a time, and in some of their prints they bade
us, look at home! that was no argument in favor
of the wisdom of wantonly rebuilding St. Mark's
façade: but certainly those of us who have not yet
looked at home in this matter had better do so

speedily, late and over late though it be : **for**
though we have no golden-pictured interiors like
St. Mark's Church at home, we still have many
buildings which are both works of ancient art and
monuments of history : and just think what is
happening to them, and note, since we profess to
recognize their value, how helpless art is in the
Century of Commerce !

In the first place, many and many a beautiful
and ancient building is being destroyed all over
civilized Europe as well as in England, because it
is supposed to interfere with the convenience of
the citizens, while a little forethought might save
it without trenching on that convenience ;* but
even apart from that, I say that if we are not
prepared to put up with a little inconvenience in
our lifetimes for the sake of preserving a monument of art which will elevate and educate, not only
ourselves, but our sons, and our sons' sons, it is
vain and idle of us to talk about art — or education
either.   Brutality must be bred of such brutality.

The same thing may be said about enlarging,

---

* As I correct these sheets for the press, the case of two such
pieces of destruction is forced upon me : first, the remains of the
Refectory of Westminster Abbey, with the adjacent Ashburnham
House, a beautiful work, probably by Inigo Jones; and second,
Magdalen Bridge at Oxford.   Certainly this seems to mock my
hope of the influence of education on the Beauty of Life; since
the first scheme of destruction is eagerly pressed forward by the
authorities of Westminster School, the second scarcely opposed
by the resident members of the University of Oxford.

or otherwise altering for convenience' sake, old buildings still in use for something like their original purposes : in almost all such cases it is really nothing more than a question of a little money for a new site ; and then a new building can be built exactly fitted for the uses it is needed for, with such art about it as our own days can furnish ; while the old monument is left to tell its tale of change and progress, to hold out example and warning to us in the practice of the arts : and thus the convenience of the public, the progress of modern art, and the cause of education, are all furthered at once at the cost of a little money.

Surely if it be worth while troubling ourselves about the works of art of to-day, of which any amount almost can be done, since we are yet alive, it is worth while spending a little care, forethought, and money in preserving the art of by-gone ages, of which (woe worth the while!) so little is left, and of which we can never have any more, whatever good-hap the world may attain to.

No man who consents to the destruction or the mutilation of an ancient building has any right to pretend that he cares about art ; or has any excuse to plead in defence of his crime against civilization and progress, save sheer brutal ignorance.

But before I leave this subject I must say a word or two about the curious invention of our own days called Restoration, a method of dealing with works of by-gone days which, though not so degrading in its spirit as downright destruction, is nevertheless little better in its results on the condition of those works of art : it is obvious that I have no time to argue the question out to-night, so I will only make these assertions :

That ancient buildings, being both works of art and monuments of history, must obviously be treated with great care and delicacy ; that the imitative art of to-day is not, and cannot be the same thing as ancient art, and cannot replace it ; and that therefore if we superimpose this work on the old, we destroy it both as art and as a record of history ; lastly, that the natural weathering of the surface of a building is beautiful, and its loss disastrous.

Now the restorers hold the exact contrary of all this : they think that any clever architect to-day can deal off-hand successfully with the ancient work ; that while all things else have changed about us since (say) the thirteenth century, art has not changed, and that our workmen can turn out work identical with that of the thirteenth century ; and, lastly, that the weather-beaten surface of an ancient building is worthless, and to be got rid of wherever possible.

You see the question is difficult to argue, because there seem to be no common grounds between the restorers and the anti-restorers : I appeal therefore to the public, and bid them note, that though our opinions may be wrong, the action we advise is not

rash : let the question be shelved awhile : if, as
we are always pressing on people, due care be
taken of these monuments, so that they shall not
fall into disrepair, they will be always there to
'restore' whenever people think proper and when
we are proved wrong ; but if it should turn out
that we are right, how can the 'restored' buildings
be restored ? I beg of you therefore to let the
question be shelved, till art has so advanced among
us, that we can deal authoritatively with it, till there
is no longer any doubt about the matter.

Surely these monuments of our art and history,
which, whatever the lawyers may say, belong not
to a coterie, or to a rich man here and there, but
to the nation at large, are worth this delay : surely
the last relics of the life of the 'famous men and
our fathers that begat us' may justly claim of us
the exercise of a little patience.

It will give us trouble no doubt, all this care of
our possessions : but there is more trouble to come ;
for I must now speak of something else, of possessions which should be common to all of us, of the
green grass, and the leaves, and the waters, of the
very light and air of heaven, which the Century of
Commerce has been too busy to pay any heed to.
And first let me remind you that I am supposing
every one here present professes to care about art.

Well, there are some rich men among us whom
we oddly enough call manufacturers, by which we
mean capitalists who pay other men to organize

manufactures; these gentlemen, many of whom
buy pictures and profess to care about art, burn
a deal of coal; there is an act in existence which
was passed to prevent them sometimes and in some
places from pouring a dense cloud of smoke over
the world, and, to my thinking, a very lame and
partial act it is: but nothing hinders these lovers
of art from being a law to themselves, and making
it a point of honor with them to minimize the smoke
nuisance as far as their own works are concerned ,
and if they don't do so, when mere money, and even
a very little of that, is what it will cost them, I
say that their love of art is a mere pretence: how
can you care about the image of a landscape when
you show by your deeds that you don't care for the
landscape itself? or what right have you to shut
yourself up with beautiful form and color when you
make it impossible for other people to have any
share in these things?

Well, and as to the smoke act itself: I don't
know what heed you pay to it in Birmingham,* but
I have seen myself what heed is paid to it in other
places; Bradford for instance: though close by them
at Saltaire they have an example which I should
have thought might have shamed them; for the
huge chimney there which serves the acres of weaving and spinning sheds of Sir Titus Salt and his

* Since perhaps some people may read these words who are
not of Birmingham, I ought to say that it was authoritatively ex-
plained at the meeting to which I addressed these words, that in
Birmingham the law is strictly enforced.

brothers is as guiltless of smoke as an ordinary
kitchen chimney. Or Manchester : a gentleman of
that city told me that the smoke-act was a mere
dead letter there : well, they buy pictures in Manchester and profess to wish to further the arts ; but
you see it must be idle pretence as far as their rich
people are concerned : they only want to talk about
it, and have themselves talked of.

I don't know what you are doing about this
matter here ; but you must forgive my saying, that
unless you are beginning to think of some way of
dealing with it, you are not beginning yet to pave
your way to success in the arts.

Well, I have spoken of a huge nuisance, which is
a type of the worst nuisances of what an ill-tempered
man might be excused for calling the Century of
Nuisances, rather than the Century of Commerce.
I will now leave it to the consciences of the rich and
influential among us, and speak of a minor nuisance
which it is in the power of every one of us to abate,
and which, small as it is, is so vexatious, that if I
can prevail on a score of you to take heed to it by
what I am saying, I shall think my evening's work
a good one. Sandwich-papers I mean — of course
you laugh ; but come now, don't you, civilized as
you are in Birmingham, leave them all about the
Lickey hills and your public gardens and the like ?
If you don't, I really scarcely know with what words
to praise you. When we Londoners go to enjoy
ourselves at Hampton Court, for instance, we take

special good care to let everybody know that we
have had something to eat ; so that the park just
outside the gates (and a beautiful place it is) looks
as if it had been snowing dirty paper.   I really
think you might promise me one and all who are
here present to have done with this sluttish habit,
which is the type of many another in its way, just
as the smoke-nuisance is.   I mean such things as
scrawling one's name on monuments, tearing down
tree boughs, and the like.

I suppose 't is early days in the revival of the
arts to express one's disgust at the daily increasing
hideousness of the posters with which all our towns
are daubed.   Still we ought to be disgusted at such
horrors, and I think make up our minds never to
buy any of the articles so advertised.   I can't believe they can be worth much if they need all that
shouting to sell them.

Again, I must ask what do you do with the trees
on a site that is going to be built over ? do you try
to save them, to adapt your houses at all to them ?
do you understand what treasures they are in a
town or a suburb ? or what a relief they will be to
the hideous dog-holes which (forgive me !) you are
probably going to build in their places ?   I ask this
anxiously, and with grief in my soul, for in London
and its suburbs we always * begin by clearing a site

* Not *quite* always : in the little colony at Bedford Park, Chis-
wick, as many trees have been left as possible, to the boundless
advantage of its quaint and pretty architecture.

till it is as bare as the pavement: I really think that almost anybody would have been shocked, if I could have shown him some of the trees that have been wantonly murdered in the suburb in which I live (Hammersmith to wit), amongst them some of those magnificent cedars, for which we along the river used to be famous once.

But here again see how helpless those are who care about art or nature amidst the hurry of the Century of Commerce.

Pray do not forget, that any one who cuts down a tree wantonly or carelessly, especially in a great town or its suburbs, need make no pretence of caring about art.

What else can we do to help to educate ourselves and others in the path of art, to be on the road to attaining an *Art made by the people and for the people as a joy to the maker and the user?*

Why, having got to understand something of what art was, having got to look upon its ancient monuments as friends that can tell us something of times bygone, and whose faces we do not wish to alter, even though they be worn by time and grief: having got to spend money and trouble upon matters of decency, great and little; having made it clear that we really do care about nature even in the suburbs of a big town — having got so far, we shall begin to think of the houses in which we live.

For I must tell you that unless you are resolved

to have good and rational architecture, it is, once
again, useless your thinking about art at all.

I have spoken of the popular arts, but they
might all be summed up in that one word Architecture; they are all parts of that great whole, and
the art of house-building begins it all: if we did
not know how to dye or to weave; if we had
neither gold, nor silver, nor silk; and no pigments to paint with, but half-a-dozen ochres and
umbers, we might yet frame a worthy art that
would lead to everything, if we had but timber,
stone, and lime, and a few cutting tools to make
these common things not only shelter us from wind
and weather, but also express the thoughts and
aspirations that stir in us.

Architecture would lead us to all the arts, as it
did with earlier men: but if we despise it and take
no note of how we are housed, the other arts will
have a hard time of it indeed.

Now I do not think the greatest of optimists
would deny that, taking us one and all, we are at
present housed in a perfectly shameful way, and
since the greatest part of us have to live in houses
already built for us, it must be admitted that it is
rather hard to know what to do, beyond waiting
till they tumble about our ears.

Only we must not lay the fault upon the builders,
as some people seem inclined to do: they are our
very humble servants, and will build what we ask
for: remember, that rich men are not obliged to

live in ugly houses, and yet you see they do; which the builders may be well excused for taking as a sign of what is wanted.

Well, the point is we must do what we can, and make people understand what we want them to do for us, by letting them see what we do for ourselves.

Hitherto, judging us by that standard, the build ers may well say, that we want the pretence of a thing rather than the thing itself; that we want a show of petty luxury if we are unrich, a show of insulting stupidity if we are rich : and they are quite clear that as a rule we want to get something that shall look as if it cost twice as much as it really did.

You cannot have Architecture on those terms : simplicity and solidity are the very first requisites of it : just think if it is not so : How we please ourselves with an old building by thinking of all the generations of men that have passed through it ! Do we not remember how it has received their joy, and borne their sorrow, and not even their folly has left sourness upon it ? It still looks as kind to us, as it did to them. And the converse of this we ought to feel when we look at a newly-built house if it were as it should be : we should feel a pleasure in thinking how he who had built it had left a piece of his soul behind him to greet the new-comers one after another long and long after he was gone : — but what sentiment can an ordinary modern house move in us, or what thought — save a hope that we may speedily forget its base ugliness?

But if you ask me how we are to pay for this solidity and extra expense, that seems to me a reasonable question ; for you must dismiss at once as a delusion the hope that has been sometimes cherished, that you can have a building which is a work of art, and is therefore above all things properly built, at the same price as a building which only pretends to be this : never forget when people talk about cheap art in general, by the way, that all art costs time, trouble, and thought, and that money is only a counter to represent these things.

However I must try to answer the question I have supposed put, how are we to pay for decent houses?

It seems to me that by a great piece of good luck the way to pay for them, is by doing that which alone can produce popular art among us : living a simple life, I mean.   Once more I say that the greatest foe to art is luxury, art cannot live in its atmosphere.

When you hear of the luxuries of the ancients, you must remember that they were not like our luxuries, they were rather indulgence in pieces of extravagant folly than what we to-day call luxury ; which perhaps you would rather call comfort : well, I accept the word, and say that a Greek or Roman of the luxurious time would stare astonished could he be brought back again, and shown the comforts of a well-to-do middle-class house.

But some, I know, think that the attainment of these very comforts is what makes the difference between civilization and uncivilization, that they are the essence of civilization. Is it so indeed? Farewell my hope then! — I had thought that civilization meant the attainment of peace and order and freedom, of good-will between man and man, of the love of truth, and the hatred of injustice, and by consequence the attainment of the good life which these things breed, a life free from craven fear, but full of incident: that was what I thought it meant, not more stuffed chairs and more cushions, and more carpets and gas, and more dainty meat and drink — and therewithal more and sharper differences between class and class.

If that be what it is, I for my part wish I were well out of it, and living in a tent in the Persian desert, or a turf hut on the Iceland hill-side. But however it be, and I think my view is the true view, I tell you that art abhors that side of civilization, she cannot breathe in the houses that lie under its stuffy slavery.

Believe me if we want art to begin at home, as it must, we must clear our houses of troublesome superfluities that are for ever in our way: conventional comforts that are no real comforts, and do but make work for servants and doctors: if you want a golden rule that will fit everybody, this is it:

'*Have nothing in your houses that you do not know to be useful, or believe to be beautiful.*'

And if we apply that rule strictly, we shall in the first place show the builders and such-like ser-vants of the public what we really want, we shall create a demand for real art, as the phrase goes; and in the second place, we shall surely have more money to pay for decent houses.

Perhaps it will not try your patience too much if I lay before you my idea of the fittings necessary to the sitting-room of a healthy person: a room, I mean, which he would not have to cook in much, or sleep in generally, or in which he would not have to do any very litter-making manual work.

First a book-case with a great many books in it: next a table that will keep steady when you write or work at it: then several chairs that you can move, and a bench that you can sit or lie upon: next a cupboard with drawers: next, unless either the book-case or the cupboard be very beautiful with painting or carving, you will want pictures or engravings, such as you can afford, only not stop-gaps, but real works of art on the wall; or else the wall itself must be ornamented with some beautiful and restful pattern: we shall also want a vase or two to put flowers in, which latter you must have sometimes, especially if you live in a town. Then there will be the fireplace of course, which in our climate is bound to be the chief object in the room.

That is all we shall want, especially if the floor be good ; if it be not, as, by the way, in a modern house it is pretty certain not to be, I admit that a small carpet which can be bundled out of the room in two minutes will be useful, and we must also take care that it is beautiful, or it will annoy us terribly.

Now unless we are musical, and need a piano (in which case, as far as beauty is concerned, we are in a bad way), that is quite all we want : and we can add very little to these necessaries without troubling ourselves, and hindering our work, our thought, and our rest.

If these things were done at the least cost for which they could be done well and solidly, they ought not to cost much ; and they are so few, that those that could afford to have them at all, could afford to spend some trouble to get them fitting and beautiful : and all those who care about art ought to take great trouble to do so, and to take care that there be no sham art amongst them, nothing that it has degraded a man to make or sell. And I feel sure, that if all who care about art were to take this pains, it would make a great impression upon the public.

This simplicity you may make as costly as you please or can, on the other hand : you may hang your walls with tapestry instead of whitewash or paper ; or you may cover them with mosaic, or have them frescoed by a great painter : all this is not luxury, if it be done for beauty's sake, and not for show : it does not break our golden rule : *Have nothing in your houses which you do not know to be useful or believe to be beautiful.*

All art starts from this simplicity ; and the higher the art rises, the greater the simplicity. I have been speaking of the fittings of a dwelling-house ; a place in which we eat and drink, and pass familiar hours ; but when you come to places which people want to make more specially beautiful because of the solemnity or dignity of their uses, they will be simpler still, and have little in them save the bare walls made as beautiful as may be. St. Mark's at Venice has very little furniture in it, much less than most Roman Catholic churches : its lovely and stately mother St. Sophia of Constantinople had less still, even when it was a Christian Church : but we need not go either to Venice or Stamboul to take note of that : go into one of our own mighty Gothic naves (do any of you remember the first time you did so ?) and note how the huge free space satisfies and elevates you, even now when window and wall are stripped of ornament : then think of the meaning of simplicity, and absence of encumbering gew-gaws.

Now after all, for us who are learning art, it is not far to seek what is the surest way to further it : that which most breeds art is art : every piece of work that we do which is well done, is so much help to the cause ; every piece of pretence and

half-heartedness is so much hurt to it : most of
you who take to the practice of art can find out
in no very long time whether you have any gifts
for it or not : if you have not, throw the thing up,
or you will have a wretched time of it yourselves,
and will be damaging the cause by laborious pretence : but if you have gifts of any kind you are
happy indeed beyond most men ; for your pleasure
is always with you, nor can you be intemperate in
the enjoyment of it, and as you use it, it does not
lessen, but grows : if you are by chance weary of it
at night, you get up in the morning eager for it; or
if perhaps in the morning it seems folly to you for
a while, yet presently, when your hand has been
moving a little in its wonted way, fresh hope has
sprung up beneath it and you are happy again.
While others are getting through the day like plants
thrust into the earth, which cannot turn this way
or that but as the wind blows them, you know what
you want, and your will is on the alert to find it,
and you, whatever happens, whether it be joy or
grief, are at least alive.

Now when I spoke to you last year, after I had
sat down I was half afraid that I had on some
points said too much, that I had spoken too
bitterly in my eagerness; that a rash word might
have discouraged some of you: I was very far
from meaning that : what I wanted to do, what I
want to do to-night is to put definitely before you
a cause for which to strive.

That cause is the Democracy of Art, the ennobling of daily and common work, which will one day put hope and pleasure in the place of fear and pain, as the forces which move men to labor and keep the world a-going.

If I have enlisted any one in that cause, rash as my words may have been, or feeble as they may have been, they have done more good than harm ; nor do I believe that any words of mine can discourage any who have joined that cause or are ready to do so : their way is too clear before them for that, and every one of us can help the cause whether he be great or little.

I know indeed that men, wearied by the pettiness of the details of the strife, their patience tried by hope deferred, will at whiles, excusably enough, turn back in their hearts to other days, when, if the issues were not clearer, the means of trying them were simpler ; when, so stirring were the times, one might even have atoned for many a blunder and backsliding by visibly dying for the cause : to have breasted the Spanish pikes at Leyden, to have drawn sword with Oliver : that may well seem to us at times amidst the tangles of to-day a happy fate : for a man to be able to say, I have lived like a fool, but now I will cast away fooling for an hour, and die like a man — there is something in that certainly : and yet 't is clear that few men can be so lucky as to die for a cause, without having first of all lived for it. And as this is the most that can be asked from the greatest man that follows a cause, so it is the least that can be taken from the smallest.

So to us who have a Cause at heart, our highest ambition and our simplest duty are one and the same thing: for the most part we shall be too busy doing the work that lies ready to our hands, to let impatience for visibly great progress vex us much; but surely since we are servants of a Cause, hope must be ever with us, and sometimes perhaps it will so quicken our vision that it will out-run the slow lapse of time, and show us the victorious days when millions of those who now sit in darkness will be enlightened by an *Art made by the people and for the people, a joy to the maker and the user.*

8

MAKING THE BEST OF IT.

I HAVE to-night to talk to you about certain things which my experience in my own craft has led me to notice, and which have bred in my mind something like a set of rules or maxims, which guide my practice. Every one who has followed a craft for long has such rules in his mind, and cannot help following them himself, and insisting on them practically in dealing with his pupils or workmen if he is in any degree a master; and when these rules, or if you will, impulses, are filling the minds and guiding the hands of many craftsmen at one time, they are busy forming a distinct school, and the art they represent is sure to be at least alive, however rude, timid, or lacking it may be; and the more imperious these rules are, the wider these impulses are spread, the more vigorously alive will be the art they produce; whereas in times when they are felt but lightly and rarely, when one man's maxims seem absurd or trivial to his brother craftsman, art is either sick or slumbering, or so thinly scattered amongst the great mass of men as to influence the general life of the world little or nothing.

For though this kind of rules of a craft may seem to some arbitrary, I think that it is because they are the result of such intricate combinations of circumstances, that only a great philosopher, if even he, could express in words the sources of them, and give us reasons for them all, and we who are craftsmen must be content to prove them in practice, believing that their roots are founded in human nature, even as we know that their firstfruits are to be found in that most wonderful of all histories, the history of the arts.

Will you, therefore, look upon me as a craftsman who shares certain impulses with many others, which impulses forbid him to question the rules they have forced on him? so looking on me you may afford perhaps to be more indulgent to me if I seem to dogmatize over much.

Yet I cannot claim to represent any one craft. The division of labor, which has played so great a part in furthering competitive commerce, till it has become a machine with powers both reproductive and destructive, which few dare to resist, and none can control or foresee the result of, has pressed specially hard on that part of the field of human culture in which I was born to labor. That field of the arts, whose harvest should be the chief part of human joy, hope, and consolation, has been, I say, dealt hardly with by the division of labor, once the servant, and now the master of competitive commerce, itself once the servant, and now the

master of civilization ; nay, so searching has been
this tyranny, that it has not passed by my own insignificant corner of labor, but as it has thwarted
me in many ways, so chiefly perhaps in this, that
it has so stood in the way of my getting the help
from others which my art forces me to crave, that
I have been compelled to learn many crafts, and
belike, according to the proverb, forbidden to master any, so that I fear my lecture will seem to you
both to run over too many things and not to go
deep enough into any.

I cannot help it.   That above-mentioned tyranny
has turned some of us from being, as we should be,
contented craftsmen, into being discontented agita-
tors against it, so that our minds are not at rest,
even when we have to talk over workshop receipts
and maxims ; indeed I must confess that I should
hold my peace on all matters connected with the
arts, if I had not a lurking hope to stir up both
others and myself to discontent with and rebellion
against things as they are, clinging to the further
hope that our discontent may be fruitful and our
rebellion steadfast, at least to the end of our own
lives, since we believe that we are rebels not against
the laws of Nature, but the customs of folly.

Nevertheless, since even rebels desire to live,
and since even they must sometimes crave for rest
and peace — nay, since they must, as it were, make
for themselves strongholds from whence to carry on
the strife — we ought not to be accused of incon-

sistency, if to-night we consider how to make the best of it. By what forethought, pains, and patience, can we make endurable those strange dwellings — the basest, the ugliest, and the most inconvenient that men have ever built for themselves, and which our own haste, necessity, and stupidity, compel almost all of us to live in? That is our present question.

In dealing with this subject, I shall perforce be chiefly speaking of those middle-class dwellings of which I know most; but what I have to say will be as applicable to any other kind; for there is no dignity or unity of plan about any modern house, big or little. It has neither centre nor individuality, but is invariably a congeries of rooms tumbled together by chance hap. So that the unit I have to speak of is a room rather than a house.

Now there may be some here who have the good luck to dwell in those noble buildings which our forefathers built, out of their very souls, one may say; such good luck I call about the greatest that can befall a man in these days. But these happy people have little to do with our troubles of to-night, save as sympathetic onlookers. All we have to do with them is to remind them not to forget their duties to those places, which they doubtless love well; not to alter them or torment them to suit any passing whim or convenience, but to deal with them as if their builders, to whom they owe so much, could still be wounded by the griefs and rejoice in

the well-doing of their ancient homes. Surely if
they do this, they also will neither be forgotten
nor unthanked in the time to come.

There may be others here who dwell in houses
that can scarcely be called noble — nay, as com-
pared with the last-named kind, may be almost
called ignoble — but their builders still had some
traditions left them of the times of art. They are
built solidly and conscientiously at least, and if
they have little or no beauty, yet have a certain
common-sense and convenience about them; nor
do they fail to represent the manners and feelings
of their own time. The earliest of these, built
about the reign of Queen Anne, stretch out a
hand toward the Gothic times, and are not without picturesqueness, especially when their surroundings are beautiful. The latest built in the
latter days of the Georges are certainly quite guiltless of picturesqueness, but are, as above said, solid,
and not inconvenient. All these houses, both the
so-called Queen Anne ones and the distinctively
Georgian, are difficult enough to decorate, especially for those who have any leaning toward romance, because they have still some style left in
them which one cannot ignore; at the same time
that it is impossible for any one living out of the
time in which they were built to sympathize with
a style whose characteristics are mere whims, not
founded on any principle. Still they are at the
worst not aggressively ugly or base, and it is pos-

sible to live in them without serious disturbance to our work or thoughts ; so that by the force of contrast they have become bright spots in the prevailing darkness of ugliness that has covered all modern life.

But we must not forget that that rebellion which we have met here, I hope, to further, has begun, and to-day shows visible tokens of its life ; for of late there have been houses rising up among us here and there which have certainly not been planned either by the common cut-and-dried designers for builders, or by academical imitators of bygone styles. Though they may be called experimental, no one can say that they are not born of thought and principle, as well as of great capacity for design. It is nowise our business to-night to criticise them. I suspect their authors, who have gone through so many difficulties (not of their own breeding) in producing them know their shortcomings much better than we can do, and are less elated by their successes than we are. At any rate, they are gifts to our country which will always be respected, whether the times better or worsen, and I call upon you to thank their designers most heartily for their forethought, labor, and hope.

Well, I have spoken of three qualifications to that degradation of our dwellings which characterizes this period of history only.

First, there are the very few houses which have been left us from the times of art. Except that we may sometimes have the pleasure of seeing these, we most of us have little enough to do with them.

Secondly, there are those houses of the times when, though art was sick and all but dead, men had not quite given it up as a bad job, and at any rate had not learned systematic bad building; and when, moreover, they had what they wanted, and their lives were expressed by their architecture. Of these there are still left a good many all over the country, but they are lessening fast before the irresistible force of competition, and will soon be very rare indeed.

Thirdly, there are a few houses built and mostly inhabited by the ringleaders of the rebellion against sordid ugliness, which we are met here to further to-night. It is clear that as yet these are very few, or you could never have thought it worth your while to come here to hear the simple words I have to say to you on this subject.

Now, these are the exceptions. The rest is what really amounts to the dwellings of all our people, which are built without any hope of beauty or care for it — without any thought that there can be any pleasure in the look of an ordinary dwelling-house, and also (in consequence of this neglect of manliness) with scarce any heed to real convenience. It will, I hope, one day be hard to believe that such houses were built for a people not lacking in honesty, in independence of life, in elevation of thought, and consideration for others; not a whit of all that do they express, but rather hypocrisy, flunkyism, and careless selfishness. The fact is, they are no longer part of our lives. We have given it up as a bad job. We are heedless if our houses express nothing of us but the very worst side of our character both national and personal.

This unmanly heedlessness, so injurious to civilization, so unjust to those that are to follow us, is the very thing we want to shake people out of. We want to make them think about their homes, to take the trouble to turn them into dwellings fit for people free in mind and body — much might come of that I think.

Now, to my mind, the first step towards this end is, to follow the fashion of our nation, so often, so *very* often, called practical, and leaving for a little an ideal scarce conceivable, to try to get people to bethink them of what we can best do with those makeshifts which we cannot get rid of all at once.

I know that those lesser arts, by which alone this can be done, are looked upon by many wise and witty people as not worth the notice of a sensible man ; but, since I am addressing a society of artists, I believe I am speaking to people who have got beyond even that stage of wisdom and wit, and that you think all the arts of importance. Yet, indeed, I should think I had but little claim on your attention if I deemed the question involved nothing save the gain of a little more content and a little more pleasure for those who already have abundance of content and pleasure ; let me say it, that either I have erred in the aim of my whole life, or that the welfare of these lesser arts involves the question of the content and self-respect of all craftsmen, whether you call them artists or artisans. So I say again, my hope is that those who begin to consider carefully how to make the best of the chambers in which they eat and sleep and study, and hold converse with their friends, will breed in their minds a wholesome and fruitful discontent with the sordidness that even when they have done their best will surround their island of comfort, and that as they try to appease this discontent they will find that there is no way out of it but by insisting that all men's work shall be fit for free men and not for machines : my extravagant hope is that people will some day learn something of art, and so long for more, and will find, as I have, that there is no getting it save by the general acknowledgment of the right of every man to have fit work to do in a beautiful home. Therein lies all that is indestructible of the pleasure of life ; no man need ask for more than that, no man should be granted less ; and if he falls short of it, it is through waste and injustice that he is kept out of his birthright.

And now I will try what I can do in my hints on this making the best of it, first asking your pardon for this, that I shall have to give a great deal

of negative advice, and be always saying 'don't'—
that, as you know, being much the lot of those who
profess reform.

Before we go inside our house, nay, before we
look at its outside, we may consider its garden,
chiefly with reference to town gardening ; which,
indeed, I, in common, I suppose, with most others
who have tried it, have found uphill work enough
— all the more as in our part of the world few indeed have any mercy upon the one thing necessary
for decent life in a town, its trees ; till we have
come to this, that one trembles at the very sound
of an axe as one sits at one's work at home. However, uphill work or not, the town garden must not
be neglected if we are to be in earnest in making
the best of it.

Now I am bound to say town gardeners generally do rather the reverse of that : our suburban
gardeners in London, for instance, oftenest wind
about their little bit of gravel walk and grass plot
in ridiculous imitation of an ugly big garden of the
landscape-gardening style, and then with a strange
perversity fill up the spaces with the most formal
plants they can get ; whereas the merest common
sense should have taught them to lay out their
morsel of ground in the simplest way, to fence it as
orderly as might be, one part from the other (if it be
big enough for that) and the whole from the road,
and then to fill up the flower-growing space with
things that are free and interesting in their growth,

leaving nature to do the desired complexity, which she will certainly not fail to do if we do not desert her for the florist, who, I must say, has made it harder work than it should be to get the best of flowers.

It is scarcely a digression to note his way of dealing with flowers, which, moreover, gives us an apt illustration of that change without thought of beauty, change for the sake of change, which has played such a great part in the degradation of art in all times. So I ask you to note the way he has treated the rose, for instance : the rose has been grown double from I don't know when ; the double rose was a gain to the world, a new beauty was given us by it, and nothing taken away, since the wild rose grows in every hedge. Yet even then one might be excused for thinking that the wild rose was scarce improved on, for nothing can be more beautiful in general growth or in detail than a way-side bush of it, nor can any scent be as sweet and pure as its scent. Nevertheless the garden rose had a new beauty of abundant form, while its leaves had not lost the wonderfully delicate texture of the wild one. The full color it had gained, from the blush rose to the damask, was pure and true amidst all its added force, and though its scent had certainly lost some of the sweetness of the eglantine, it was fresh still, as well as so abundantly rich. Well, all that lasted till quite our own day, when the florists fell upon the rose — men who could never have enough — they strove for size and got it, a fine specimen of a florist's rose being about as big as a moderate Savoy cabbage. They tried for strong scent and got it — till a florist's rose has not unseldom a suspicion of the scent of the aforesaid cabbage — not at its best. They tried for strong color, and got it, strong and bad — like a conqueror. But all this while they missed the very essence of the rose's being ; they thought there was nothing in it but redundance and luxury ; they exaggerated these into coarseness, while they threw away the exquisite subtility of form, delicacy of texture, and sweetness of color, which, blent with the richness which the true garden rose shares with many other flowers, yet makes it the queen of them all — the flower of flowers. Indeed, the worst of this is that these sham roses are driving the real ones out of existence. If we do not look to it our descendants will know nothing of the cabbage rose, the loveliest in form of all, or the blush rose with its dark green stems and unequalled color, or the yellow-centred rose of the East, which carries the richness of scent to the very furthest point it can go without losing freshness : they will know nothing of all these, and I fear they will reproach the poets of past time for having done according to their wont, and exaggerated grossly the beauties of the rose.

Well, as a Londoner perhaps I have said too much of roses, since we can scarcely grow them among suburban smoke ; but what I have said of them applies to other flowers, of which I will say this much more. Be very shy of double flowers ; choose the old columbine where the clustering doves are unmistakable and distinct, not the double one, where they run into mere tatters. Choose (if you can get it) the old china-aster with the yellow centre, that goes so well with the purple-brown stems and curiously colored florets, instead of the lumps that look like cut paper, of which we are now so proud. Don't be swindled out of that wonder of beauty, a single snowdrop ; there is no gain and plenty of loss in the double one. More loss still in the double sunflower, which is a coarse-colored and dull plant, whereas the single one, though a late comer to our gardens, is by no means to be despised, since it will grow anywhere, and is both interesting and beautiful, with its sharply chiselled yellow florets relieved by the quaintly patterned sad-colored centre clogged with honey and beset with bees and butterflies.

So much for over-artificiality in flowers. A word or two about the misplacing of them. Don't have ferns in your garden. The hart's-tongue in the clefts of the rock, the queer things that grow within reach of the spray of the waterfall ; these are right in their places. Still more the brake on the woodside, whether in late autumn, when its withered haulm helps out the well-remembered woodland scent, or in spring, when it is thrusting its volutes through last year's waste. But all this is nothing to a garden, and is not to be got out of it; and if you try it you will take away from it all possible romance, the romance of a garden.

The same thing may be said about many plants, which are curiosities only, which Nature meant to be grotesque, not beautiful, and which are generally the growth of hot countries, where things sprout over quick and rank. Take note that the strangest of these come from the jungle and the tropical waste, from places where man is not at home, but is an intruder, an enemy. Go to a botanical garden and look at them, and think of those strange places to your heart's content. But don't set them to starve in your smoke-drenched scrap of ground amongst the bricks, for they will be no ornament to it.

As to color in gardens. Flowers in masses are mighty strong color, and if not used with a great deal of caution are very destructive to pleasure in gardening. On the whole, I think the best and safest plan is to mix up your flowers, and rather eschew great masses of color — in combination I mean. But there are some flowers (inventions of men, *i.e.* florists) which are bad color altogether, and not to be used at all. Scarlet geraniums, for instance, or the yellow calceolaria, which indeed are not uncommonly grown together profusely, in order, I suppose, to show that even flowers can be thoroughly ugly.

Another thing also much too commonly seen is
an aberration of the human mind, which otherwise
I should have been ashamed to warn you of. It is
technically called carpet-gardening. Need I explain
it further? I had rather not, for when I think of it
even when I am quite alone I blush with shame at
the thought.

I am afraid it is specially necessary in these days
when making the best of it is a hard job, and when
the ordinary iron hurdles are so common and so
destructive of any kind of beauty in a garden, to
say when you fence anything in a garden use a live
hedge, or stones set flatwise (as they do in some
parts of the Cotswold country), or timber, or wattle,
or, in short, anything but iron.*

And now to sum up as to a garden. Large or
small, it should look both orderly and rich. It
should be well fenced from the outside world. It
should by no means imitate either the wilfulness or
the wildness of Nature, but should look like a thing
never to be seen except near a house. It should,
in fact, look like a part of the house. It follows
from this that no private pleasure-garden should be
very big, and a public garden should be divided and
made to look like so many flower-closes in a meadow, or a wood, or amidst the pavement.

---

* I know that well-designed hammered iron trellises and gates
have been used happily enough, though chiefly in rather grandiose
gardens, and so they might be again — one of these days — but I
fear not yet awhile.

It will be a key to right thinking about gardens if you consider in what kind of places a garden is most desired. In a very beautiful country, especially if it be mountainous, we can do without it well enough ; whereas in a flat and dull country we crave after it, and there it is often the very making of the homestead. While in great towns, gardens, both private and public, are positive necessities if the citizens are to live reasonable and healthy lives in body and mind.

So much for the garden, of which, since I have said that it ought to be part of the house, I hope I have not spoken too much.

Now, as to the outside of our makeshift house, I fear it is too ugly to keep us long. Let what painting you have to do about it be as simple as possible, and be chiefly white or whitish ; for when a building is ugly in form it will bear no decoration, and to mark its parts by varying color will be the way to bring out its ugliness. So I don't advise you to paint your houses blood-red and chocolate with white facings, as seems to be getting the fashion in some parts of London. You should, however, always paint your sash-bars and window-frames white to break up the dreary space of window somewhat. The only other thing I have to say, is to warn you against using at all a hot brownish-red, which some decorators are very fond of. Till some one invents a better name for it, let us call it cockroach color, and have nought to do with it.

9

So we have got to the inside of our house, and
are in the room we have to live in, call it by what
name you will. As to its proportions, it will be
great luck indeed in an ordinary modern house if
they are tolerable ; but let us hope for the best. If
it is to be well proportioned, one of its parts, either
its height, length, or breadth, ought to exceed the
others, or be marked somehow. If it be square, or
so nearly as to seem so, it should not be high ; if it
be long and narrow, it might be high without any
harm, but yet would be more interesting low ;
whereas if it be an obvious but moderate oblong
on plan, great height will be decidedly good.

As to the parts of a room that we have to think
of, they are wall, ceiling, floor, windows and doors,
fireplace, and movables. Of these the wall is of so
much the most importance to a decorator, and will
lead us so far afield that I will mostly clear off the
other parts first, as to the mere arrangement of
them, asking you meanwhile to understand that
the greater part of what I shall be saying as to the
design of the patterns for the wall, I consider more
or less applicable to patterns everywhere.

As to the windows then ; I fear we must grumble
again. In most decent houses, or what are so called,
the windows are much too big, and let in a flood
of light in a haphazard and ill-considered way,
which the indwellers are forced to obscure again
by shutters, blinds, curtains, screens, heavy up-
holsteries, and such other nuisances. The win-

dows, also, are almost always brought too low down, and often so low down as to have their sills on a level with our ankles, sending thereby a raking light across the room that destroys all pleasantness of tone. The windows, moreover, are either big rectangular holes in the wall, or, which is worse, have ill-proportioned round or segmental heads, while the common custom in 'good' houses is either to fill these openings with one huge sheet of plate-glass, or to divide them across the middle with a thin bar. If we insist on glazing them thus, we may make up our minds that we have done the worst we can for our windows, nor can a room look tolerable where it is so treated. You may see how people feel this by their admiration of the tracery of a Gothic window, or the lattice-work of a Cairo house. Our makeshift substitute for those beauties must be the filling of the window with moderate-sized panes of glass (plate-glass if you will) set in solid sash-bars; we shall then at all events feel as if we were indoors on a cold day — as if we had a roof over our heads.

As to the floor: a little time ago it was the universal custom for those who could afford it to cover it all up into its dustiest and crookedest corners with a carpet, good bad or indifferent. Now I daresay you have heard from others, whose subject is the health of houses rather than their art (if indeed the two subjects can be considered apart, as they cannot really be), you have heard from teachers like Dr. Richardson what a nasty and unwholesome custom this is, so I will only say that it looks nasty and unwholesome. Happily, however, it is now a custom so much broken into that we may consider it doomed ; for in all houses that pretend to any taste of arrangement, the carpet is now a rug, large it may be, but at any rate not looking immovable, and not being a trap for dust in the corners. Still I would go further than this even, and get rich people no longer to look upon a carpet as a necessity for a room at all, at least in the summer. This would have two advantages : 1st. It would compel us to have better floors (and less drafty), our present ones being one of the chief disgraces to modern building ; and 2ndly, since we should have less carpet to provide, what we did have we could afford to have better. We could have a few real works of art at the same price for which we now have hundreds of yards of makeshift machine-woven goods. In any case it is a great comfort to see the actual floor ; and the said floor may be, as you know, made very ornamental by either wood mosaic, or tile and marble mosaic ; the latter especially is such an easy art as far as mere technicality goes, and so full of resources, that I think it is a great pity it is not used more. The contrast between its gray tones and the rich positive color of Eastern carpet-work is so beautiful, that the two together make satisfactory decoration for a room with little addition.

When wood mosaic or parquet-work is used, owing to the necessary simplicity of the forms, I think it best not to vary the color of the wood. The variation caused by the diverse lie of the grain and so forth, is enough. Most decorators will be willing, I believe, to accept it as an axiom, that when a pattern is made up of very simple geometrical forms, strong contrast of color is to be avoided.

So much for the floor. As for its fellow, the ceiling, that is, I must confess, a sore point with me in my attempts at making the best of it. The simplest and most natural way of decorating a ceiling is to show the under side of the joists and beams duly moulded, and, if you will, painted in patterns. How far this is from being possible in our modern makeshift houses, I suppose I need not say. Then there is a natural and beautiful way of ornamenting a ceiling by working the plaster into delicate patterns, such as you see in our Elizabethan and Jacobean houses ; which often enough, richly designed and skilfully wrought as they are, are by no means pedantically smooth in finish — nay, may sometimes be called rough as to workmanship. But, unhappily there are few of the lesser arts that have fallen so low as the plasterers'. The cast work one sees perpetually in pretentious rooms is a mere ghastly caricature of ornament, which no one is expected to look at if he can help it. It is simply meant to say, 'This house is built for a rich man.'

The very material of it is all wrong, as, indeed, mostly happens with an art that has fallen sick. That richly designed, freely wrought plastering of our old houses was done with a slowly drying tough plaster, that encouraged the hand like modeller's clay, and could not have been done at all with the brittle plaster used in ceilings now-a-days, whose excellence is supposed to consist in its smoothness only.   To be good, according to our present false standard, it must shine like a sheet of hot-pressed paper, so that, for the present, and without the expenditure of abundant time and trouble, this kind of ceiling decoration is not to be hoped for.

It may be suggested that we should paper our ceilings like our walls, but I can't think that it will do.   Theoretically, a paper-hanging is so much distemper color applied to a surface by being printed on paper instead of being painted on plaster by the hand ; but practically, we never forget that it is paper, and a room papered all over would be like a box to live in.   Besides, the covering a room all over with cheap recurring patterns in an uninteresting material, is but a poor way out of our difficulty, and one which we should soon tire of.

There remains, then, nothing but to paint our ceilings cautiously and with as much refinement as we can, when we can afford it: though even that simple matter is complicated by the hideousness of the aforesaid plaster ornaments and cornices, which are so very bad that you must ignore them by leaving them unpainted, though even this neglect, while you paint the flat of the ceiling, makes them in a way part of the decoration, and so is apt to beat you out of every scheme of color conceivable. Still, I see nothing for it but cautious painting, or leaving the blank white space alone, to be forgotten if possible. This painting, of course, assumes that you know better than to use gas in your rooms, which will indeed soon reduce all your decorations to a pretty general average.

So now we come to the walls of our room, the part which chiefly concerns us, since no one will admit the possibility of leaving them quite alone. And the first question is, how shall we space them out horizontally?

If the room be small and not high, or the wall be much broken by pictures and tall pieces of furniture, I would not divide it horizontally. One pattern of paper, or whatever it may be, or one tint may serve us, unless we have in hand an elaborate and architectural scheme of decoration, as in a makeshift house is not like to be the case; but if it be a good-sized room, and the wall be not much broken up, some horizontal division is good, even if the room be not very high.

How are we to divide it then? I need scarcely say not into two equal parts; no one out of the island of Laputa could do that. For the rest, unless again we have a very elaborate scheme of decoration, I think dividing it once, making it into

two spaces, is enough. Now there are practically
two ways of doing that: you may either have a
narrow frieze below the cornice, and hang the wall
thence to the floor, or you may have a moderate
dado, say 4 feet 6 inches high, and hang the wall
from the cornice to the top of the dado. Either
way is good, according to circumstances ; the first
with the tall hanging and the narrow frieze is fittest
if your wall is to be covered with stuffs, tapestry,
or panelling, in which case making the frieze a
piece of delicate painting is desirable in default of
such plaster-work as I have spoken of above ; or
even if the proportions of the room very much cry
out for it, you may, in default of hand-painting, use
a strip of printed paper, though this, I must say, is
a makeshift of makeshifts.   The division into dado,
and wall hung from thence to the cornice, is fittest
for a wall which is to be covered with painted
decoration, or its makeshift, paper-hangings.

As to these, I would earnestly dissuade you from
using more than one pattern in one room, unless
one of them be but a breaking of the surface with a
pattern so insignificant as scarce to be noticeable.
I have seen a good deal of the practice of putting
pattern over pattern in paper-hangings, and it seems
to me a very unsatisfactory one, and I am, in short,
convinced, as I hinted just now, that cheap recurring patterns in a material which has no play of
light in it, and no special beauty of its own, should
be employed rather sparingly, or they destroy all

refinement of decoration and blunt our enjoyment of whatever beauty may lie in the designs of such things.

Before I leave this subject of the spacing out of the wall for decoration, I should say that in dealing with a very high room it is best to put nothing that attracts the eye above the level of about eight feet from the floor — to let everything above that be mere air and space, as it were. I think you will find that this will tend to take off that look of dreariness that often besets tall rooms.

So much, then, for the spacing out of our wall. We have now to consider what the covering of it is to be, which subject, before we have done with it, will take us over a great deal of ground and lead us into the consideration of designing for flat spaces in general with work other than picture work.

To clear the way, I have a word or two to say about the treatment of the woodwork in our room. If I could I would have no woodwork in it that needed flat-painting, meaning by that word a mere paying it over with four coats of tinted lead-pigment ground in oils or varnish, but unless one can have a noble wood, such as oak, I don't see what else is to be done. I have never seen deal stained transparently with success, and its natural color is poor, and will not enter into any scheme of decoration, while polishing it makes it worse. In short, it is such a poor material that it must be hidden unless it be used on a big scale as mere timber. Even then, in a church-roof or what not, coloring it with distemper will not hurt it, and in a room I should certainly do this to the woodwork of roof and ceiling, while I painted such woodwork as came within touch of hand.   As to the color of this, it should, as a rule, be of the same general tone as the walls, but a shade or two darker in tint.   Very dark woodwork makes a room dreary and disagreeable, while unless the decoration be in a very bright key of color, it does not do to have the woodwork lighter than the walls.   For the rest, if you are lucky enough to be able to use oak, and plenty of it, found your decoration on that, leaving it just as it comes from the plane.

Now, as you are not bound to use anything for the decoration of your walls but simple tints, I will here say a few words on the main colors, before I go on to what is more properly decoration, only in speaking of them one can scarce think only of such tints as are fit to color a wall with, of which, to say truth, there are not many.

Though we may each have our special preferences among the main colors, which we shall do quite right to indulge, it is a sign of disease in an artist to have a prejudice against any particular color, though such prejudices are common and violent enough among people imperfectly educated in art, or with naturally dull perceptions of it.   Still, colors have their ways in decoration, so to say, both positively in themselves, and relatively to each

man's way of using them. So I may be excused
for setting down some things I seem to have noticed
about those ways.

Yellow is not a color that can be used in
masses unless it be much broken or mingled with
other colors, and even then it wants some material
to help it out, which has great play of light and
shade in it. You know people are always calling
yellow things golden, even when they are not at all
the color of gold, which, even unalloyed, is not a
bright yellow. That shows that delightful yellows
are not very positive, and that, as aforesaid, they
need gleaming materials to help them. The light
bright yellows, like jonquil and primrose, are
scarcely usable in art, save in silk, whose gleam
takes color from and adds light to the local tint,
just as sunlight does to the yellow blossoms which
are so common in Nature. In dead materials, such
as distemper color, a positive yellow can only be
used sparingly in combination with other tints.

Red is also a difficult color to use, unless it be
helped by some beauty of material, for whether it
tend toward yellow and be called scarlet, or toward blue and be crimson, there is but little pleasure in it, unless it be deep and full. If the scarlet
pass a certain degree of impurity it falls into the
hot brown-red, very disagreeable in large masses.
If the crimson be much reduced it tends towards a
cold color called in these latter days magenta, impossible for an artist to use either by itself or in

combination. The finest tint of red is a central one between crimson and scarlet, and is a very powerful color indeed, but scarce to be got in a flat tint. A crimson broken by grayish-brown, and tending towards russet, is also a very useful color, but, like all the finest reds, is rather a dyer's color than a house-painter's; the world being very rich in soluble reds, which of course are not the most enduring of pigments, though very fast as soluble colors.

Pink, though one of the most beautiful colors in combination, is not easy to use as a flat tint even over moderate spaces; the more orangy shades of it are the most useful, a cold pink being a color much to be avoided.

As to purple, no one in his senses would think of using it bright in masses. In combination it may be used somewhat bright, if it be warm and tend towards red; but the best and most characteristic shade of purple is nowise bright, but tends towards russet. Egyptian porphyry, especially when contrasted with orange, as in the pavement of St. Mark's at Venice, will represent the color for you. At the British Museum, and one or two other famous libraries, are still left specimens of this tint, as Byzantine art in its palmy days understood it. These are books written with gold and silver on vellum stained purple, probably with the now lost murex or fish-dye of the ancients, the tint of which dye-stuff Pliny describes minutely and accurately in his 'Natural History.' I need scarcely say that no ordinary flat tint could reproduce this most splendid of colors.

Though green (at all events in England) is the color widest used by Nature, yet there is not so much bright green used by her as many people seem to think ; the most of it being used for a week or two in spring, when the leafage is small, and blended with the grays and other negative colors of the twigs ; when 'leaves grow large and long,' as the ballad has it, they also grow gray. I believe it has been noted by Mr. Ruskin, and it certainly seems true, that the pleasure we take in the young spring foliage comes largely from its tenderness of tone rather than its brightness of hue. Anyhow, you may be sure that if we try to outdo Nature's green tints on our walls we shall fail, and make ourselves uncomfortable to boot. We must, in short, be very careful of bright greens, and seldom, if ever, use them at once bright and strong.

On the other hand, do not fall into the trap of a dingy bilious-looking yellow-green, a color to which I have special and personal hatred, because (if you will excuse my mentioning personal matters) I have been supposed to have somewhat brought it into vogue. I assure you I am not really responsible for it.

The truth is, that to get a green that is at once pure and neither cold nor rank, and not too bright to live with, is of simple things as difficult as anything a decorator has to do ; but it can be done, and without the help of special material ; and when done such a green is so useful, and so restful to the eyes, that in this matter also we are bound to follow Nature and make large use of that work-a-day color green.

But if green be called a work-a-day color, surely blue must be called the holiday one, and those who long most for bright colors may please themselves most with it ; for if you duly guard against getting it cold if it tend towards red, or rank if it tend towards green, you need not be much afraid of its brightness.   Now, as red is above all a dyer's color, so blue is especially a pigment and an enamel color ; the world is rich in insoluble blues, many of which are practically indestructible.

I have said that there are not many tints fit to color a wall with : this is my list of them as far as I know ; a solid red, not very deep, but rather describable as a full pink, and toned both with yellow and blue, a very fine color if you can hit it ; a light orangy pink, to be used rather sparingly. A pale golden tint, *i.e.*, a yellowish brown ; a very difficult color to hit.   A color between these two last, call it pale copper color.   All these three you must be careful over, for if you get them muddy or dirty you are lost.

Tints of green from pure and pale to deepish and gray : always remembering that the purer the paler, and the deeper the grayer.

Tints of pure pale blue from a greenish one, the color of a starling's egg, to a gray ultramarine color, hard to use because so full of color, but incomparable when right. In these you must carefully avoid the point at which the green overcomes the blue and turns it rank, or that at which the red overcomes the blue and produces those woful hues of pale lavender and starch blue which have not seldom been favorites with decorators of elegant drawing-rooms and respectable dining-rooms.

You will understand that I am here speaking of distemper tinting, and in that material these are all the tints I can think of; if you use bolder, deeper, or stronger colors I think you will find yourself beaten out of monochrome in order to get your color harmonious.

One last word as to distemper which is not monochrome, and its makeshift, paper-hanging. I think it always best not to force the color, but to be content with getting it either quite light or quite gray in these materials, and in no case very dark, trusting for richness to stuffs, or to painting which allows of gilding' being introduced.

I must finish these crude notes about general color by reminding you that you must be moderate with your color on the walls of an ordinary dwelling-room ; according to the material you are using you may go along the scale from light and bright to deep and rich, but some soberness of tone is absolutely necessary if you would not weary people

till they cry out against all decoration. But I suppose this is a caution which only very young decorators are likely to need.   It is the right-hand
defection ; the left-hand falling away is to get your
color dingy and muddy, a worse fault than the other,
because less likely to be curable.   All right-minded
craftsmen who work in color will strive to make
their work as bright as possible, as full of color as
the nature of the work will allow it to be.   The
meaning they may be bound to express, the nature
of its material, or the use it may be put to may
limit this fulness ; but in whatever key of color
they are working, if they do not succeed in getting
the color pure and clear, they have not learned
their craft, and if they do not see their fault when
it is present in their work they are not likely to
learn it.

Now, hitherto we have not got further into the
matter of decoration than to talk of its arrangement.
Before I speak of some general matters connected
with our subject, I must say a little on the design
of the patterns which will form the chief part of
your decoration.   The subject is a wide and difficult
one, and my time much too short to do it any justice, but here and there, perhaps, a hint may crop
up, and I may put it in a way somewhat new.

On the whole, in speaking of these patterns I
shall be thinking of those that necessarily recur ;
designs which have to be carried out by more or
less mechanical appliances, such as the printing-
block or the loom.

Since we have been considering color lately, we had better take that side first, though I know it will be difficult to separate the consideration of it from that of the other necessary qualifications of design.

The first step away from monochrome is breaking the ground by putting a pattern on it of the same color, but of a lighter or darker shade, the first being the best and most natural way. I need say but little on this as a matter of color, though many very important designs are so treated. One thing I have noticed about these damasks, as I should call them ; that of the three chief colors, red is the one where the two shades must be the nearest to one another, or you get the effect poor and weak ; while in blue you may have a great deal of difference without losing color, and green holds a middle place between the two.

Next, if you make these two shades different in tint as well as, or instead of, in depth, you have fairly got out of monochrome, and will find plenty of difficulties in getting your two tints to go well together. The putting, for instance, of a light greenish blue on a deep reddish one, turquoise on sapphire, will try all your skill. The Persians practise this feat, but not often without adding a third color, and so getting into the next stage. In fact, this plan of relieving the pattern by shifting its tint as well as its depth, is chiefly of use in dealing with quite low-toned colors — golden browns or grays,

for instance.   In dealing with the more forcible
ones, you will find it in general necessary to add
a third color at least, and so get into the next
stage.

This is the relieving a pattern of more than one
color, but all the colors light upon a dark ground.
This is above all useful in cases where your palette
is somewhat limited ; say, for instance, in a figured
cloth which has to be woven mechanically, and
where you have but three or four colors in a line,
including the ground.

You will not find this a difficult way of relieving
your pattern, if you only are not too ambitious of
getting the diverse superimposed colors too forcible on the one hand, so that they fly out from one
another, or on the other hand too delicate, so that
they run together into confusion.   The excellence
of this sort of work lies in a clear but soft relief of
the form, in colors each beautiful in itself, and harmonious one with the other on a ground whose color
is also beautiful, though unobtrusive.   Hardness
ruins the work, confusion of form caused by timidity
of color annoys the eye, and makes it restless, and
lack of color is felt as destroying the *raison d'être* of
it.   So you see it taxes the designer heavily enough
after all.   Nevertheless I still call it the easiest way
of complete pattern-designing.

I have spoken of it as the placing of a light pattern on dark ground.   I should mention that in the
fully developed form of the design I am thinking

of there is often an impression given, of there being more than one plane in the pattern. Where the pattern is strictly on one plane, we have not reached the full development of this manner of designing, the full development of color and form used to-gether, but form predominant.

We are not left without examples of this kind of design at its best. The looms of Corinth, Palermo, and Lucca, in the twelfth, thirteenth, and fourteenth centuries, turned out figured silk cloths, which were so widely sought for, that you may see specimens of their work figured on fifteenth-century screens in East Anglian churches, or the back-ground of pictures by the Van Eyks, while one of the most important collections of the actual goods is preserved in the treasury of the Mary Church at Dantzig ; the South Kensington Museum has also a very fine collection of these, which I can't help thinking are not quite as visible to the public as they should be. They are, however, discoverable by the help of Dr. Rock's excellent catalogue pub-lished by the department, and I hope will, as the Museum gains space, be more easy to see.

Now to sum up : This method of pattern-design-ing must be considered the Western and civilized method ; that used by craftsmen who were always seeing pictures, and whose minds were full of defi-nite ideas of form. Color was essential to their work, and they loved it, and understood it, but always subordinated it to form.

There is next the method of relief by placing a dark figure on a light ground. Sometimes this method is but the converse of the last, and is not so useful, because it is capable of less variety and play of color and tone. Sometimes it must be looked on as a transition from the last-mentioned method to the next of color laid by color. Thus used there is something incomplete about it. One finds oneself longing for more colors than one's shuttles or blocks allow one. There is a need felt for the specialty of the next method, where the dividing line is used, and it gradually gets drawn into that method. Which, indeed, is the last I have to speak to you of, and in which color is laid by color.

In this method it is necessary that the diverse colors should be separated each by a line of another color, and that not merely to mark the form, but to complete the color itself; which outlining, while it serves the purpose of gradation, which in more naturalistic work is got by shading, makes the design quite flat, and takes from it any idea of there being more than one plane in it.

This way of treating pattern design is so much more difficult than the others, as to be almost an art by itself, and to demand a study apart. As the method of relief by laying light upon dark may be called the Western way of treatment and the civilized, so this is the Eastern, and, to a certain extent, the uncivilized.

But it has a wide range, from works where the form is of little importance and only exists to make boundaries for color, to those in which the form is so studied, so elaborate, and so lovely, that it is hardly true to say that the form is subordinate to the color ; while on the other hand, so much delight is taken in the color, it is so inventive and so unerringly harmonious, that it is scarcely possible to think of the form without it — the two inter-penetrate.

Such things as these, which, as far as I know, are only found in Persian art at its best, do carry the art of mere pattern-designing to its utmost perfection, and it seems somewhat hard to call such an art uncivilized. But, you see, its whole soul was given up to producing matters of sub-sidiary art, as people call it ; its carpets were of more importance than its pictures ; nay, properly speaking, they were its pictures. And it may be that such an art never has a future of change be-fore it, save the change of death, which has now certainly come over that Eastern art ; while the more impatient, more aspiring, less sensuous art which belongs to Western civilization may bear many a change and not die utterly ; nay, may feed on its intellect alone for a season, and enduring the martyrdom of a grim time of ugliness, may live on, rebuking at once the narrow-minded pedant of science, and the luxurious tyrant of plu-tocracy, till change bring back the spring again, and it blossoms once more into pleasure. May it be so.

Meanwhile, we may say for certain that color for color's sake only will never take real hold on the art of our civilization, not even in its subsidiary art. Imitation and affectation may deceive people into thinking that such an instinct is quickening amongst us, but the deception will not last. To have a meaning and to make others feel and understand it, must ever be the aim and end of our Western art.

Before I leave this subject of the coloring of patterns, I must warn you against the abuse of the dotting, hatching, and lining of backgrounds, and other mechanical contrivances for breaking them ; such practices are too often the resource to which want of invention is driven, and unless used with great caution they vulgarize a pattern completely. Compare, for instance, those Sicilian and other silk cloths I have mentioned with the brocades (common everywhere), turned out from the looms of Lyons, Venice, and Genoa, at the end of the seventeenth and beginning of the eighteenth centuries. The first perfectly simple in manufacture, trusting wholly to beauty of design, and the play of light on the naturally woven surface, while the latter eke out their gaudy feebleness with spots and ribs and long floats, and all kinds of meaningless tormenting of the web, till there is nothing to be learned from them save a warning.

So much for the color of pattern-designing
Now, for a space, let us consider some other things
that are necessary to it, and which I am driven to
call its moral qualities, and which are finally re-
ducible to two — order and meaning.

Without order your work cannot even exist ;
without meaning, it were better not to exist.

Now order imposes on us certain limitations,
which partly spring from the nature of the art itself,
and partly from the materials in which we have to
work ; and it is a sign of mere incompetence in
either a school or an individual to refuse to accept
such limitations, or even not to accept them joyfully
and turn them to special account, much as if a poet
should complain of having to write in measure and
rhyme.

Now, in our craft the chief of the limitations
that spring from the essence of the art is that the
decorator's art cannot be imitative even to the
limited extent that the picture-painter's art is.

This you have been told hundreds of times, and
in theory it is accepted everywhere, so I need not
say much about it — chiefly this, that it does not
excuse want of observation of nature, or laziness of
drawing, as some people seem to think. On the
contrary, unless you know plenty about the natural
form that you are conventionalizing, you will not
only find it impossible to give people a satisfactory
impression of what is in your own mind about it,
but you will also be so hampered by your ignorance,

that you will not be able to make your conventionalized form ornamental. It will not fill a space properly, or look crisp and sharp, or fulfil any purpose you may strive to put it to.

It follows from this that your convention must be your own, and not borrowed from other times and peoples; or, at the least, that you must make it your own by thoroughly understanding both the nature and the art you are dealing with. If you do not heed this, I do not know but what you may not as well turn to and draw laborious portraits of natural forms of flower and bird and beast, and stick them on your walls anyhow. It is true you will not get ornament so, but you may learn something for your trouble; whereas, using an obviously true principle as a stalking-horse for laziness of purpose and lack of invention, will but injure art all round, and blind people to the truth of that very principle.

Limitations also, both as to imitation and exuberance, are imposed on us by the office our pattern has to fulfil. A small and often-recurring pattern of a subordinate kind will bear much less naturalism than one in a freer space and more important position, and the more obvious the geometrical structure of a pattern is, the less its parts should tend toward naturalism. This has been well understood from the earliest days of art to the very latest times during which pattern-designing has clung to any wholesome tradition, but is pretty generally unheeded at present.

As to the limitations that arise from the material we may be working in, we must remember that all material offers certain difficulties to be overcome, and certain facilities to be made the most of. Up to a certain point you must be the master of your material, but you must never be so much the master as to turn it surly, so to say. You must not make it your slave, or presently you will be a slave also. You must master it so far as to make it express a meaning, and to serve your aim at beauty. You may go beyond that necessary point for your own pleasure and amusement, and still be in the right way; but if you go on after that merely to make people stare at your dexterity in dealing with a difficult thing, you have forgotten art along with the rights of your material, and you will make not a work of art, but a mere toy; you are no longer an artist, but a juggler. The history of the arts gives us abundant examples and warnings in this matter. First clear steady principle, then playing with the danger, and lastly falling into the snare, mark with the utmost distinctness the times of the health, the decline and the last sickness of art.

Allow me to give you one example in the noble art of mosaic. The difficulty in it necessary to be overcome was the making of a pure and true flexible line, not over thick, with little bits of glass or marble nearly rectangular. Its glory lay in its durability, the lovely color to be got in it, the play

of light on its faceted and gleaming surface, and
the clearness mingled with softness, with which
forms were relieved on the lustrous gold which was
so freely used in its best days.   Moreover, however
bright were the colors used, they were toned de-
lightfully by the grayness which the innumerable
joints between the tesseræ spread over the whole
surface.

Now the difficulty of the art was overcome in
its earliest and best days, and no care or pains
were spared in making the most of its special
qualities, while for long and long no force was put
upon the material to make it imitate the qualities
of brush-painting, either in power of color, in
delicacy of gradation, or intricacy of treating a
subject ; and, moreover, easy as it would have been
to minimize the jointing of the tesseræ, no attempt
was made at it.

But as time went on, men began to tire of the
solemn simplicity of the art, and began to aim at
making it keep pace with the growing complexity
of picture painting, and, though still beautiful, it
lost color without gaining form.   From that point
(say about 1460), it went on from bad to worse, till
at last men were set to work in it merely because
it was an intractable material in which to imitate
oil-painting, and by this time it was fallen from
being a master art, the crowning beauty of the
most solemn buildings, to being a mere tax on
the craftsmen's patience, and a toy for people who

no longer cared for art. And just such a history may be told of every art that deals with special material.

Under this head of order should be included something about the structure of patterns, but time for dealing with such an intricate question obviously fails me ; so I will but note that, whereas it has been said that a recurring pattern should be constructed on a geometrical basis, it is clear that it cannot be constructed otherwise ; only the structure may be more or less masked, and some designers take a great deal of pains to do so.

I cannot say that I think this always necessary. It may be so when the pattern is on a very small scale, and meant to attract but little attention. But it is sometimes the reverse of desirable in large and important patterns, and, to my mind, all noble patterns should at least *look* large. Some of the finest and pleasantest of these show their geometrical structure clearly enough ; and if the lines of them grow strongly and flow gracefully, I think they are decidedly helped by their structure not being elaborately concealed.

At the same time in all patterns which are meant to fill the eye and satisfy the mind, there should be a certain mystery. We should not be able to read the whole thing at once, nor desire to do so, nor be impelled by that desire to go on tracing line after line to find out how the pattern is made, and I think that the obvious presence of a geometrical order, if it be, as it should be, beautiful, tends towards this end, and prevents our feeling restless over a pattern.

That every line in a pattern should have its due growth, and be traceable to its beginning, this, which you have doubtless heard before, is undoubtedly essential to the finest pattern work; equally so is it that no stem should be so far from its parent stock as to look weak or wavering. Mutual support and unceasing progress distinguish real and natural order from its mockery, pedantic tyranny.

Every one who has practised the designing of patterns knows the necessity for covering the ground equably and richly. This is really to a great extent the secret of obtaining the look of satisfying mystery aforesaid, and it is the very test of capacity in a designer.

Finally, no amount of delicacy is too great in drawing the curves of a pattern, no amount of care in getting the leading lines right from the first, can be thrown away, for beauty of detail cannot afterwards cure any shortcoming in this. Remember that a pattern is either right or wrong. It cannot be forgiven for blundering, as a picture may be which has otherwise great qualities in it. It is with a pattern as with a fortress, it is no stronger than its weakest point. A failure for ever recurring torments the eye too much to allow the mind to take any pleasure in suggestion and intention.

As to the second moral quality of design, mean-ing, I include in that the invention and imagination which forms the soul of this art, as of all others, and which, when submitted to the bonds of order, has a body and a visible existence.

Now you may well think that there is less to be said of this than the other quality; for form may be taught, but the spirit that breathes through it cannot be. So I will content myself with saying this on these qualities, that though a designer may put all manner of strangeness and surprise into his patterns, he must not do so at the expense of beauty. You will never find a case in this kind of work where ugliness and violence are not the result of barrenness, and not of fertility of inven-tion. The fertile man, he of resource, has not to worry himself about invention. He need but think of beauty and simplicity of expression; his work will grow on and on, one thing leading to another, as it fares with a beautiful tree. Whereas the laborious paste and scissors man goes hunting up and down for oddities, sticks one in here and another there, and tries to connect them with commonplace; and when it is all done, the oddities are not more inventive than the commonplace, nor the commonplace more graceful than the oddities.

No pattern should be without some sort of meaning. True it is that that meaning may have come down to us traditionally, and not be our own

invention, yet we must at heart understand it, or
we can neither receive it, nor hand it down to our
successors.   It is no longer tradition if it is ser-
vilely copied, without change, the token of life.
You may be sure that the softest and loveliest of
patterns will weary the steadiest admirers of their
school as soon as they see that there is no hope of
growth in them.   For you know all art is compact
of effort, of failure, and of hope, and we cannot but
think that somewhere perfection lies ahead, as we
look anxiously for the better thing that is to come
from the good.

Furthermore, you must not only mean something
in your patterns, but must also be able to make
others understand that meaning.   They say that
the difference between a genius and a madman is
that the genius can get one or two people to believe
in him, whereas the madman, poor fellow, has himself only for his audience.   Now the only way in
our craft of design for compelling people to understand you is to follow hard on Nature ; for what
else can you refer people to, or what else is there
which everybody can understand ? — everybody that
it is worth addressing yourself to, which includes
all people who can feel and think.

Now let us end the talk about those qualities of
invention and imagination with a word of memory
and of thanks to the designers of time past.   Surely
he who runs may read them abundantly set forth
in those lesser arts they practised.   Surely it had

been pity indeed, if so much of this had been lost as would have been if it had been crushed out by the pride of intellect, that will not stoop to look at beauty, unless its own kings and great men have had a hand in it. Belike the thoughts of the men who wrought this kind of art could not have been expressed in grander ways or more definitely, or, at least, would not have been ; therefore I believe I am not thinking only of my own pleasure, but of the pleasure of many people, when I praise the usefulness of the lives of these men, whose names are long forgotten, but whose works we still wonder at. In their own way they meant to tell us how the flowers grew in the gardens of Damascus, or how the hunt was up on the plains of Kirman, or how the tulips shone among the grass in the Mid-Persian valley, and how their souls delighted in it all, and what joy they had in life ; nor did they fail to make their meaning clear to some of us.

But, indeed, they and other matters have led us afar from our makeshift house, and the room we have to decorate therein. And there is still left the fireplace to consider.

Now I think there is nothing about a house in which a contrast is greater between old and new than this piece of architecture. The old, either delightful in its comfortable simplicity, or decorated with the noblest and most meaning art in the place ; the modern, mean, miserable, uncomfortable, and showy, plastered about with wretched sham ornament, trumpery of cast-iron, and brass and polished steel, and what not — offensive to look at, and a nuisance to clean — and the whole thing huddled up with rubbish of ash-pan, and fender, and rug, till surely the hearths which we have been bidden so often to defend (whether there was a chance of their being attacked or not) have now become a mere figure of speech, the meaning of which in a short time it will be impossible for learned philologists to find out.

I do most seriously advise you to get rid of all this, or as much of it as you can without absolute ruin to your prospects in life ; and even if you do not know how to decorate it, at least have a hole in the wall of a convenient shape, faced with such bricks or tiles as will at once bear fire and clean ; then some sort of iron basket in it, and out from that a real hearth of cleanable brick or tile, which will not make you blush when you look at it, and as little in the way of guard and fender as you think will be safe ; that will do to begin with. For the rest, if you have wooden work about the fireplace, which is often good to have, don't mix up the wood and the tiles together ; let the wood-work look like part of the wall-covering, and the tiles like part of the chimney.

As for movable furniture, even if time did not fail us, 't is a large subject — or a very small one — so I will but say, don't have too much of it ; have none for mere finery's sake, or to satisfy the claims

of custom — these are flat truisms, are they not?
But really it seems as if some people had never
thought of them, for 't is almost the universal
custom to stuff up some rooms so that you can
scarcely move in them, and to leave others deadly
bare ; whereas all rooms ought to look as if they
were lived in, and to have, so to say, a friendly wel-
come ready for the incomer.

A dining-room ought not to look as if one went
into it as one does into a dentist's parlor — for an
operation, and came out of it when the operation
was over — the tooth out, or the dinner in. A drawing-room ought to look as if some kind of work could
be done in it less toilsome than being bored. A
library certainly ought to have books in it, not
boots only, as in Thackeray's country snob's house,
but so ought each and every room in the house
more or less ; also, though all rooms should look
tidy, and even very tidy, they ought not to look
too tidy.

Furthermore, no room of the richest man should
look grand enough to make a simple man shrink in
it, or luxurious enough to make a thoughtful man
feel ashamed in it ; it will not do so if art be at
home there, for she has no foes so deadly as
insolence and waste. Indeed, I fear that at present the decoration of rich men's houses is mostly
wrought out at the bidding of grandeur and luxury,
and that art has been mostly cowed or shamed out
of them ; nor when I come to think of it will I

lament it overmuch. Art was not born in the palace; rather she fell sick there, and it will take more bracing air than that of rich men's houses to heal her again. If she is ever to be strong enough to help mankind once more, she must gather strength in simple places; the refuge from wind and weather to which the goodman comes home from field or hill-side; the well-tidied space into which the craftsman draws from the litter of loom, and smithy, and bench; the scholar's island in the sea of books; the artist's clearing in the canvas-grove; it is from these places that Art must come if she is ever again to be enthroned in that other kind of building, which I think, under some name or other, whether you call it church or hall of reason, or what not, will always be needed; the building in which people meet to forget their own transient personal and family troubles in aspi rations for their fellows and the days to come, and which to a certain extent make up to town-dwellers for their loss of field, and river, and mountain.

Well, it seems to me that these two kinds of buildings are all we have really to think of, together with whatsoever outhouses, workshops, and the like may be necessary. Surely the rest may quietly drop to pieces for aught we care. Unless it should be thought good in the interest of history to keep one standing in each big town to show posterity what strange, ugly, uncomfortable houses rich men dwelt in once upon a time.

Meantime now, when rich men won't have art, and poor men can't, there is, nevertheless, some unthinking craving for it, some restless feeling in men's minds of something lacking somewhere, which has made many benevolent people seek for the possibility of cheap art.

What do they mean by that? One art for the rich and another for the poor? No, it won't do. Art is not so accommodating as the justice or religion of society, and she won't have it.

What then? There has been cheap art at some times certainly, at the expense of the starvation of the craftsmen. But people can't mean that; and if they did would, happily, no longer have the same chance of getting it that they once had. Still they think art can be got round some way or other — jockeyed, so to say. I rather think in this fashion: that a highly gifted and carefully educated man shall, like Mr. Pecksniff, squint at a sheet of paper, and that the results of that squint shall set a vast number of well-fed, contented operatives (they are ashamed to call them workmen) turning crank handles for ten hours a-day, bidding them keep what gifts and education they may have been born with for their — I was going to say leisure hours, but I don't know how to, for if I were to work ten hours a-day at work I despised and hated, I should spend my leisure I hope in political agitation, but I fear — in drinking. So let us say that the aforesaid operatives will have to keep their inborn gifts and education for their dreams. Well, from this system are to come threefold blessings — food and clothing, poorish lodging and a little leisure to the operatives, enormous riches to the capitalists that rent them, together with moderate riches to the squinter on the paper ; and lastly, very decidedly lastly, abundance of cheap art for the operatives or crank turners to buy — in their dreams.

Well, there have been many other benevolent and economical schemes for keeping your cake after you have eaten it, for skinning a flint, and boiling a flea down for its tallow and glue, and this one of cheap art may just go its way with the others.

Yet to my mind real art is cheap, even at the price that must be paid for it. That price is, in short, the providing of a handicraftsman who shall put his own individual intelligence and enthusiasm into the goods he fashions. So far from his labor being 'divided,' which is the technical phrase for his always doing one minute piece of work, and never being allowed to think of any other ; so far from that, he must know all about the ware he is making and its relation to similar wares ; he must have a natural aptitude for his work so strong, that no education can force him away from his special bent. He must be allowed to think of what he is doing, and to vary his work as the circumstances of it vary, and his own moods. He must be for ever striving to make the piece he is at work at better than the last. He must refuse at anybody's

bidding to turn out, I won't say a bad, but even an
indifferent piece of work, whatever the public want,
or think they want. He must have a voice, and a
voice worth listening to, in the whole affair.

Such a man I should call, not an operative, but
a workman. You may call him an artist if you
will, for I have been describing the qualities of
artists, as I know them ; but a capitalist will be
apt to call him a ' troublesome fellow,' a radical of
radicals, and, in fact, he will be troublesome —
mere grit and friction in the wheels of the money-
grinding machine.

Yes, such a man will stop the machine perhaps ;
but it is only through him that you can have art,
i. e. civilization unmaimed, if you really want it ; so
consider, if you do want it, and will pay the price,
and give the workman his due.

What is his due ? that is, what can he take
from you, and be the man that you want? Money
enough to keep him from fear of want or degradation for him and his ; leisure enough from bread-
earning work (even though it be pleasant to him)
to give him time to read and think, and connect
his own life with the life of the great world ; work
enough of the kind aforesaid, and praise of it, and
encouragement enough to make him feel good
friends with his fellows ; and lastly (not least, for
't is verily part of the bargain), his own due share
of art, the chief part of which will be a dwelling
that does not lack the beauty which Nature would

freely allow it, if our own perversity did not turn nature out of doors.

That is the bargain to be struck, such work and such wages ; and I believe that if the world wants the work and is willing to pay the wages, the workmen will not long be wanting.

On the other hand, if it be certain that the world — that is, modern civilized society — will nevermore ask for such workmen, then I am as sure as that I stand here breathing, that art is dying : that the spark still smouldering is not to be quickened into life, but damped into death.   And indeed, often, in my fear of that, I think 'would that I could see what is to take the place of art !'   For, whether modern civilized society *can* make that bargain aforesaid, who shall say ?   I know well — who could fail to know it ? — that the difficulties are great.

Too apt has the world ever been, 'for the sake of life to cast away the reasons for living,' and perhaps is more and more apt to it as the conditions of life get more intricate, as the race to avoid ruin, which seems always imminent and overwhelming, gets swifter and more terrible.   Yet how would it be if we were to lay aside fear and turn in the face of all that, and stand by our claim to have, one and all of us, reasons for living?   Mayhap the heavens would not fall on us if we did.

Anyhow, let us make up our minds which we want, art, or the absence of art, and be prepared if we want art, to give up many things, and in many ways to change the conditions of life. Perhaps there are those who will understand me when I say that that necessary change may make life poorer for the rich, rougher for the refined, and, it may be, duller for the gifted — for a while; that it may even take such forms that not the best or wisest of us shall always be able to know it for a friend, but may at whiles fight against it as a foe. Yet, when the day comes that gives us visible token of art rising like the sun from below — when it is no longer a justly despised whim of the rich, or a lazy habit of the so-called educated, but a thing that labor begins to crave as a necessity, even as labor is a necessity for all men — in that day how shall all trouble be forgotten, all folly forgiven — even our own!

Little by little it must come, I know. Patience and prudence must not be lacking to us, but courage still less. Let us be a Gideon's band. 'Whosoever is fearful and afraid, let him return, and depart early from Mount Gilead.' And among that band let there be no delusions ; let the last encouraging lie have been told, the last after-dinner humbug spoken, for surely though the days seem dark, we may remember that men longed for freedom while yet they were slaves ; that it was in times when swords were reddened every day that men began to think of peace and order, and to strive to win them.

We who think, and can enjoy the feast that
Nature has spread for us, is it not both our right
and our duty to rebel against that slavery of the
waste of life's joys, which people thoughtless and
joyless, by no fault of their own, have wrapped the
world in? From our own selves we can tell that
there is hope of victory in our rebellion, since we
have art enough in our lives, not to content us,
but to make us long for more, and that longing
drives us into trying to spread art and the longing
for art ; and as it is with us so it will be with those
that we win over: little by little, we may well
hope, will do its work, till at last a great many
men will have enough of art to see how little they
have, and how much they might better their lives,
if every man had his due share of art — that is,
just so much as he could use if a fair chance were
given him.

Is that, indeed, too extravagant a hope? Have
you not heard how it has gone with many a cause
before now? First, few men heed it ; next, most
men contemn it ; lastly, all men accept it — and
the cause is won.

THE PROSPECTS OF ARCHITECTURE IN CIVILIZATION.

'—— the horrible doctrine that this universe is a Cockney Nightmare — which no creature ought for a moment to believe or listen to.' — THOMAS CARLYLE.

THE word Architecture has, I suppose, to most of you the meaning of the art of building nobly and ornamentally. Now, I believe the practice of this art to be one of the most important things which man can turn his hand to, and the consideration of it to be worth the attention of serious people, not for an hour only, but for a good part of their lives, even though they may not have to do with it professionally.

But, noble as that art is by itself, and though it is specially the art of civilization, it neither ever has existed nor ever can exist alive and progressive by itself, but must cherish and be cherished by all the crafts whereby men make the things which they intend shall be beautiful, and shall last somewhat beyond the passing day.

It is this union of the arts, mutually helpful and harmoniously subordinated one to another, which I have learned to think of as Architecture, and when I use the word to-night, that is what I shall mean by it, and nothing narrower.

A great subject truly, for it embraces the consideration of the whole external surroundings of the life of man; we cannot escape from it if we would so long as we are part of civilization, for it means the moulding and altering to human needs of the very face of the earth itself, except in the outermost desert.

Neither can we hand over our interests in it to a little band of learned men, and bid them seek and discover, and fashion, that we may at last stand by and wonder at the work, and learn a little of how 't was all done : 't is we ourselves, each one of us, who must keep watch and ward over the fairness of the earth, and each with his own soul and hand do his due share therein, lest we deliver to our sons a lesser treasure than our fathers left to us.

Nor, again, is there time enough and to spare that we may leave this matter alone till our latter days or let our sons deal with it : for so busy and eager is mankind, that the desire of to-day makes us utterly forget the desire of yesterday and the gain it brought ; and whensoever in any object of pursuit we cease to long for perfection, corruption sure and speedy leads from life to death, and all is soon over and forgotten : time enough there may be for many things : for peopling the desert ; for breaking down the walls between nation and nation; for learning the innermost secrets of the fashion of our souls and bodies, the air we breathe, and the earth we tread on: time enough for subduing all the forces of nature to our material wants: but no time to spare before we turn our eyes and our longing to the fairness of the earth ; lest the wave of human need sweep over it and make it not a hopeful desert as it once was, but a hopeless prison: lest man should find at last that he has toiled and striven, and conquered, and set all things on the earth under his feet, that he might live thereon himself unhappy.

Most true it is that when any spot of earth's surface has been marred by the haste or carelessness of civilization, it is heavy work to seek a remedy, nay a work scarce conceivable ; for the desire to live on any terms which nature has implanted in us, and the terribly swift multiplication of the race which is the result of it, thrusts out of men's minds all thought of other hopes, and bars the way before us as with a wall of iron: no force but a force equal to that which marred can ever mend, or give back those ruined places to hope and civilization.

Therefore I entreat you to turn your minds to thinking of what is to come of Architecture, that is to say, the fairness of the earth amidst the habitations of men: for the hope and the fear of it will follow us though we try to escape it ; it concerns us all, and needs the help of all ; and what we do

herein must be done at once, since every day of
our neglect adds to the heap of troubles a blind
force is making for us; till it may come to this if
we do not look to it, that we shall one day have to
call, not on peace and prosperity, but on violence
and ruin to rid us of them.

In making this appeal to you, I will not suppose
that I am speaking to any who refuse to admit that
we who are part of civilization are responsible to
posterity for what may befall the fairness of the
earth in our own days, for what we have done, in
other words, towards the progress of Architecture ;
if any such exist among cultivated people, I need
not trouble myself about them ; for they would not
listen to me, nor should I know what to say to
them.

On the other hand, there may be some here who
have a knowledge of their responsibility in this matter, but to whom the duty that it involves seems
an easy one, since they are fairly satisfied with the
state of Architecture as it now is: I do not suppose that they fail to note the strange contrast
which exists between the beauty that still clings
to some habitations of men, and the ugliness which
is the rule in others, but it seems to them natural
and inevitable, and therefore does not trouble them:
and they fulfil their duties to civilization and the
arts by sometimes going to see the beautiful places,
and gathering together a few matters to remind
them of these for the adornment of the ugly dwell-

ings in which their homes are enshrined : for the
rest they have no doubt that it is natural and not
wrong that while all ancient towns, I mean towns
whose houses are largely ancient, should be beautiful and romantic, all modern ones should be ugly
and commonplace : it does not seem to them that
this contrast is of any import to civilization, or that
it expresses anything save that one town *is* ancient
as to its buildings and the other modern. If their
thoughts carry them into looking any farther into
the contrast between ancient art and modern, they
are not dissatisfied with the result : they may see
things to reform here and there, but they suppose,
or, let me say, take for granted, that art is alive
and healthy, is on the right road, and that following
that road, it will go on living for ever, much as it
is now.

It is not unfair to say that this languid complacency is the general attitude of cultivated people
towards the arts : of course if they were ever to
think seriously of them, they would be startled into
discomfort by the thought that civilization as it now
is brings inevitable ugliness with it : surely if they
thought this, they would begin to think that this
was not natural and right ; they would see that this
was not what civilization aimed at in its struggling
days : but they do not think seriously of the arts
because they have been hitherto defended by a law
of nature which forbids men to see evils which they
are not ready to redress.

Hitherto: but there are not wanting signs that that defence may fail them one day, and it has become the duty of all true artists, and all men who love life though it be troublous better than death though it be peaceful, to strive to pierce that defence and to sting the world, cultivated and uncultivated, into discontent and struggle.

Therefore I will say that the contrast between past art and present, the universal beauty of men's habitations as they *were* fashioned, and the universal ugliness of them as they *are* fashioned, is of the utmost import to civilization, and that it expresses much, it expresses no less than a blind brutality which will destroy art at least, whatever else it may leave alive : art is not healthy, it even scarcely lives ; it is on the wrong road, and if it follow that road will speedily meet its death on it.

Now perhaps you will say that by asserting that the general attitude of cultivated people towards the arts is a languid complacency with this unhealthy state of things, I am admitting that cultivated people generally do not care about the arts, and that therefore this threatened death of them will not frighten people much, even if the threat be founded on truth : so that those are but beating the air who strive to rouse people into discontent and struggle.

Well, I will run the risk of offending you by speaking plainly, and saying, that to me it seems over true that cultivated people in general do *not*

care about the arts : nevertheless I will answer any
possible challenge as to the usefulness of trying to
rouse them to thought about the matter, by saying
that they do not care about the arts because they
do not know what they mean, or what they lose in
lacking them : cultivated, that is rich, as they are,
they also are under that harrow of hard necessity
which is driven onward so remorselessly by the
competitive commerce of the latter days ; a system
which is drawing near now I hope to its perfection,
and therefore to its death and change: the many
millions of civilization, as labor is now organized,
can scarce think seriously of anything but the
means of earning their daily bread ; they do not
know of art, it does not touch their lives at all :
the few thousands of cultivated people, whom fate,
not always as kind to them as she looks, has placed
above the material necessity for this hard struggle,
are nevertheless bound by it in spirit : the reflex of
the grinding trouble of those who toil to live that
they may live to toil weighs upon them also, and
forbids them to look upon art as a matter of importance : they know it but as a toy, not as a serious help to life : as they know it, it can no more
lift the burden from the conscience of the rich, than
it can from the weariness of the poor. They do
not know what art means : as I have said, they
think as labor is now organized art can go indefi-
nitely as *it* is now organized, practised by a few
for a few, adding a little interest, a little refinement

to the lives of those who have come to look upon intellectual interest and spiritual refinement as their birthright.

No, no, it can never be: believe me if it were otherwise possible that it should be an enduring condition of humanity that there must be one class utterly refined and another utterly brutal, art would bar the way and forbid the monstrosity to exist: such refinement would have to do as well as it might without the aid of art: it may be she will die, but it cannot be that she will live the slave of the rich, and the token of the enduring slavery of the poor.   If the life of the world is to be brutalized by her death, the rich must share that brutalization with the poor.

I know that there are people of good-will now, as there have been in all ages, who have conceived of art as going hand in hand with luxury, nay, as being much the same thing ; but it is an idea false from the root up, and most hurtful to art, as I could demonstrate to you by many examples if I had time, lacking which I will only meet it with one, which I hope will be enough.

We are here in the richest city of the richest country of the richest age of the world : no luxury of time past can compare with our luxury ; and yet if you could clear your eyes from habitual blindness you would have to confess that there is no crime against art, no ugliness, no vulgarity which is not shared with perfect fairness and equality between the modern hovels of Bethnal Green and the modern palaces of the West End: and then if you looked at the matter deeply and seriously you would not regret it, but rejoice at it, and as you went past some notable example of the aforesaid palaces you would exult indeed as you said, 'So that is all that luxury and money can do for refinement.'

For the rest, if of late there has been any change for the better in the prospects of the arts ; if there has been a struggle both to throw off the chains of dead and powerless tradition, and to understand the thoughts and aspirations of those among whom those traditions were once alive powerful and beneficent ; if there has been abroad any spirit of resistance to the flood of sordid ugliness that modern civilization has created to make modern civilization miserable : in a word, if any of us have had the courage to be discontented that art seems dying, and to hope for her new birth, it is because others have been discontented and hopeful in other matters than the arts : I believe most sincerely that the steady progress of those whom the stupidity of language forces me to call the lower classes in material, political and social condition, has been our real help in all that we have been able to do or to hope, although both the helpers and the helped have been mostly unconscious of it.

It is indeed in this belief, the belief in the beneficent progress of civilization, that I venture to face you and to entreat you to strive to enter into the

real meaning of the arts, which are surely the expression of reverence for nature, and the crown of
nature, the life of man upon the earth.

With this intent in view I may, I think, hope to
move you, I do not say to agree to all I urge upon
you, yet at least to think the matter worth thinking
about; and if you once do that, I believe I shall
have won you.   Maybe indeed that many things
which I think beautiful you will deem of small
account; nay that even some things I think base
and ugly will not vex your eyes or your minds : but
one thing I know you will none of you like to plead
guilty to; blindness to the natural beauty of the
earth; and of that beauty art is the only possible
guardian.

No one of you can fail to know what neglect of
art has done to this great treasure of mankind : the
earth which was beautiful before man lived on it,
which for many ages grew in beauty as men grew
in numbers and power, is now growing uglier day
by day, and there the swiftest where civilization is
the mightiest : this is quite certain; no one can
deny it : are you contented that it should be so?

Surely there must be few of us to whom this
degrading change has not been brought home per-
sonally.   I think you will most of you understand
me but too well when I ask you to remember the
pang of dismay that comes on us when we revisit
some spot of country which has been specially
sympathetic to us in times past; which has re-

freshed us after toil, or soothed us after trouble ;
but where now as we turn the corner of the road or
crown the hill's brow we can see first the inevitable
blue slate roof, and then the blotched mud-colored
stucco, or ill-built wall of ill-made bricks of the new
buildings ; then as we come nearer, and see the
arid and pretentious little gardens, and cast-iron
horrors of railings, and miseries of squalid outhouses breaking through the sweet meadows and
abundant hedge-rows of our old quiet hamlet, do
not our hearts sink within us, and are we not
troubled with a perplexity not altogether selfish,
when we think what a little bit of carelessness it
takes to destroy a world of pleasure and delight,
which now whatever happens can never be re-
covered ?

Well may we feel the perplexity and sickness
of heart, which some day the whole world shall feel
to find its hopes disappointed, if we do not look to
it ; for this is not what civilization looked for : a
new house added to the old village, where is the
harm of that ? Should it not have been a gain and
not a loss ; a sign of growth and prosperity which
should have rejoiced the eye of an old friend ? a
new family come in health and hope to share the
modest pleasures and labors of the place we loved ;
that should have been no grief, but a fresh pleasure
to us.

Yes, and time was that it would have been so ·
the new house indeed would have taken away a

little piece of the flowery green sward, a few yards
of the teeming hedge-row ; but a new order, a new
beauty would have taken the place of the old : the
very flowers of the field would have but given place
to flowers fashioned by man's hand and mind : the
hedge-row oak would have blossomed into fresh
beauty in roof-tree and lintel and door-post : and
though the new house would have looked young
and trim beside the older houses and the ancient
church ; ancient even in those days ; yet it would
have a piece of history for the time to come, and
its dear and dainty cream-white walls would have
been a genuine link among the numberless links of
that long chain, whose beginnings we know not of,
but on whose mighty length even the many-pillared
garth of Pallas, and the stately dome of the Eternal
Wisdom, are but single links, wondrous and resplen-
dent though they be.

Such I say can a new house be, such it has
been : for 't is no ideal house I am thinking of : no
rare marvel of art, of which but few can ever be
vouchsafed to the best times and countries : no
palace either, not even a manor-house, but a yeoman's steading at grandest, or even his shepherd's
cottage : there they stand at this day, dozens of
them yet, in some parts of England : such an one,
and of the smallest, is before my eyes as I speak to
you, standing by the roadside on one of the western
slopes of the Cotswolds : the tops of the great trees
near it can see a long way off the mountains of the

Welsh border, and between a great county of hill, and waving woodland, and meadow and plain where lies hidden many a famous battle-field of our stout forefathers : there to the right a wavering patch of blue is the smoke of Worcester town, but Evesham smoke though near, is unseen, so small it is : then a long line of haze just traceable shows where Avon wends its way thence towards Severn, till Bredon Hill hides the sight both of it and Tewkesbury smoke : just below on either side the Broadway lie the gray houses of the village street ending with a lovely house of the fourteenth century ; above the road winds serpentine up the steep hillside, whose crest looking westward sees the glorious map I have been telling of spread before it, but eastward strains to look on Oxfordshire, and thence all waters run towards Thames : all about lie the sunny slopes, lovely of outline, flowery and sweetly grassed, dotted with the best-grown and most graceful of trees : 't is a beautiful country side indeed, not undignified, not unromantic, but most familiar.

And there stands the little house that was new once, a laborer's cottage built of the Cotswold limestone, and grown now, walls and roof, a lovely warm gray, though it was creamy white in its earliest day ; no line of it could ever have marred the Cotswold beauty ; everything about it is solid and well wrought: it is skilfully planned and well proportioned : there is a little sharp and delicate carving about its arched doorway, and every part of it is well cared for : 't is in fact beautiful, a work of art and a piece of nature — no less : there is no man who could have done it better considering its use and its place.

Who built it then ? No strange race of men, but just the mason of Broadway village : even such a man as is now running up down yonder three or four cottages of the wretched type we know too well : nor did he get an architect from London, or even Worcester, to design it : I believe 't is but two hundred years old, and at that time, though beauty still lingered among the peasants' houses, your learned architects were building houses for the high gentry that were ugly enough, though solid and well built ; nor are its materials far-fetched ; from the neighboring field came its walling stones ; and at the top of the hill they are quarrying now as good freestone as ever.

No, there was no effort or wonder about it when it was built, though its beauty makes it strange now.

And are you contented that we should lose all this ; this simple harmless beauty that was no hindrance or trouble to any man, and that added to the natural beauty of the earth instead of marring it ?

You cannot be contented with it ; all you can do is to try to forget it, and to say that such things are the necessary and inevitable consequences of

civilization. Is it so indeed? The loss of such-
like beauty is an undoubted evil : but civilization
cannot mean at heart to produce evils for mankind :
such losses therefore must be accidents of civilization, produced by its carelessness, not its malice :
and we, if we be men and not machines, must try to
amend them : or civilization itself will be undone.

But now let us leave the sunny slopes of the
Cotswolds, and their little gray houses, lest we fall
a-dreaming over past time, and let us think about
the suburbs of London, neither dull nor unpleasant
once, where surely we ought to have some power
to do something : let me remind you how it fares
with the beauty of the earth when some big house
near our dwelling-place, which has passed through
many vicissitudes of rich merchant's dwelling,
school, hospital, or what not, is at last to be turned
into ready money, and is sold to A, who lets it to
B, who is going to build houses on it which he will
sell to C, who will let them to D and the other
letters of the alphabet : well, the old house comes
down ; that was to be looked for, and perhaps you
don't much mind it ; it was never a work of art,
was stupid and unimaginative enough, though cred-
itably built, and without pretence ; but even while
it is being pulled down, you hear the axe falling on
the trees of its generous garden, which it was such
a pleasure even to pass by, and where man and
nature together have worked so long and patiently
for the blessing of the neighbors : so you see the

boys dragging about the streets great boughs of the flowering may-trees covered with blossom, and you know what is going to happen.   Next morning when you get up you look towards that great plane-tree which has been such a friend to you so long through sun and rain and wind, which was a world in itself of incident and beauty : but now there is a gap and no plane-tree; next morning 't is the turn of the great sweeping layers of darkness that the ancient cedars thrust out from them, very treasures of loveliness and romance ; they are gone too : you may have a faint hope left that the thick bank of lilac next your house may be spared, since the new-comers may like lilac ; but 't is gone in the afternoon, and the next day when you look in with a sore heart, you see that once fair great garden turned into a petty miserable clay-trampled yard, and everything is ready for the latest development of Victorian architecture — which in due time (two months) arises from the wreck.

Do you like it ?   You, I mean, who have not studied art and do not think you care about it ?

Look at the houses (there are plenty to choose from) !   I will not say, are they beautiful, for you say you don't care whether they are or not : but just look at the wretched pennyworths of material, of accommodation, of ornament doled out to you ! if there were one touch of generosity, of honest pride, of wish to please about them, I would forgive them in the lump.   But there is none — not one.

It is for this that you have sacrificed your cedars and planes and may-trees, which I do believe you really liked — are you satisfied ?

Indeed you cannot be : all you can do is to go to your business, converse with your family, eat, drink, and sleep, and try to forget it, but whenever you think of it, you will admit that a loss without compensation has befallen you and your neighbors.

Once more neglect of art has done it ; for though it is conceivable that the loss of your neighboring open space might in any case have been a loss to you, still the building of a new quarter of a town ought not to be an unmixed calamity to the neighbors : nor would it have been once : for first, the builder does n't now murder the trees (at any rate not all of them) for the trifling sum of money their corpses will bring him, but because it will take him too much trouble to fit them into the planning of his houses : so to begin with you would have saved the more part of your trees; and I say *your* trees advisedly, for they were at least as much *your* trees, who loved them and would have saved them, as they were the trees of the man who neglected and murdered them. And next, for any space you would have lost, and for any unavoidable destruction of natural growth, you would in the times of art have been compensated by orderly beauty, by visible signs of the ingenuity of man and his delight both in the works of nature and the works of his own hands.

Yes indeed, if we had lived in Venice in early days, as islet after islet was. built upon, we should have grudged it but little, I think, though we had been merchants and rich men, that the Greek shafted work, and the carving of the Lombards was drawn nearer and nearer to us and blocked us out a little from the sight of the blue Euganean hills or the Northern mountains. Nay, to come neare home, much as I know I should have loved the wil lowy meadows between the network of the streams of Thames and Cherwell ; yet I should not have been ill-content as Oxford crept northward from its early home of Oseney, and Rewley, and the Castle, as townsman's house, and scholar's hall, and the great College and the noble church hid year by year more and more of the grass and flowers o Oxfordshire.*

That was the natural course of things then ; men could do no otherwise when they built than give some gift of beauty to the world : but all is turned inside out now, and when men build they cannot but take away some gift of beauty, which nature or their own forefathers have given to the world.

Wonderful it is indeed, and perplexing, that the course of civilization towards perfection should have brought this about: so perplexing, that to some it seems as if civilization were eating her own children, and the arts first of all.

* Indeed it is a new world now, when the new Cowley dog-holes must needs slay Magdalen Bridge ! — *Nov.* 1881.

I will not say that ; time is big with so many a change : surely there must be some remedy, and whether there be or no, at least it is better to die seeking one, than to leave it alone and do nothing.

I have said, are you satisfied ? and assumed that you are not, though to many you may seem to be at least helpless : yet indeed it is something or even a great deal that I can reasonably assume that you are discontented : fifty years ago, thirty years ago, nay perhaps twenty years ago, it would have been useless to have asked such a question, it could only have been answered in one way : we are perfectly satisfied : whereas now we may at least hope that discontent will grow till some remedy will be sought for.

And if sought for, should it not, in England at least, be as good as found already, and acted upon ? At first sight it seems so truly ; for I may say without fear of contradiction that we of the English middle-classes are the most powerful body of men that the world has yet seen, and that anything we have set our heart upon we will have : and yet when we come to look the matter in the face, we cannot fail to see that even for us with all our strength it will be a hard matter to bring about that birth of the new art : for between us and that which is to be, if art is not to perish utterly, there is something alive and devouring ; something as it were a river of fire that will put all that tries to swim across to a hard proof indeed, and scare from the plunge every soul that is not made fearless by desire of truth and insight of the happy days to come beyond.

That fire is the hurry of life bred by the gradual perfection of competitive commerce which we, the English middle-classes, when we had won our political liberty, set ourselves to further with an energy, an eagerness, a single-heartedness that has no parallel in history ; we would suffer none to bar the way to us, we called on none to help us, we thought of that one thing and forgot all else, and so attained to our desire, and fashioned a terrible thing indeed from the very hearts of the strongest of mankind.

Indeed I don't suppose that the feeble discontent with our own creation that I have noted before can deal with such a force as this — not yet — not till it swells to very strong discontent : nevertheless as we were blind to its destructive power, and have not even yet learned all about *that,* so we may well be blind to what it has of constructive force in it, and that one day may give us a chance to deal with it again and turn it toward accomplishing our new and worthier desire : in that day at least when we have at last learned what we want, let us work no less strenuously and fearlessly, I will not say to quench it, but to force it to burn itself out, as we once did to quicken, and sustain it.

Meantime if we could but get ourselves ready by casting off certain old prejudices and delusions in this matter of the arts, we should the sooner reach the pitch of discontent which would drive us into action : such a one I mean as the aforesaid idea that luxury fosters art, and especially the Architectural arts ; or its companion one, that the arts flourish best in a rich country, *i. e.* a country where the contrast between rich and poor is greatest : or this, the worst because the most plausible, the assertion of the hierarchy of intellect in the arts : an old foe with a new face indeed ; born out of the times that gave the death-blow to the political and social hierarchies, and waxing as they waned, it proclaimed from a new side the divinity of the few and the subjugation of the many, and cries out, like they did, that it is expedient, not that one man should die for the people, but that the people should die for one man.

Now perhaps these three things, though they have different forms, are in fact but one thing ; tyranny to wit : but however that may be, they are to be met by one answer, and there is no other : if art which is now sick is to live and not die, it must in the future be of the people, for the people, and by the people ; it must understand all and be understood by all : equality must be the answer to tyranny : if that be not attained, art will die.

The past art of what has grown to be civilized Europe from the time of the decline of the ancient classical peoples, was the outcome of instinct working on an unbroken chain of tradition : it was fed not by knowledge but by hope, and though many a strange and wild illusion mingled with that hope, yet was it human and fruitful ever: many a man it solaced, many a slave in body it freed in soul: boundless pleasure it gave to those who wrought it and those who used it: long and long it lived, passing that torch of hope from hand to hand, while it kept but little record of its best and noblest; for least of all things could it abide to make for itself kings and tyrants: every man's hand and soul it used, the lowest as the highest, and in its bosom at least were all men free: it did its work, not creating an art more perfect than itself, but rather other things than art, freedom of thought and speech, and the longing for light and knowledge and the coming days that should slay it: and so at last it died in the hour of its highest hope, almost before the greatest men that came of it had passed away from the world. It is dead now; no longing will bring it back to us; no echo of it is left among the peoples whom it once made happy.

Of the art that is to come who may prophesy? But this at least seems to follow from comparing that past with the confusion in which we are now struggling and the light that glimmers through it: that that art will no longer be an art of instinct, of ignorance which is hopeful to learn and strives to see; since ignorance is now no longer hopeful. In this and in many other ways it may differ from the past art, but in one thing it must needs be like it; it will not be an esoteric mystery shared by a little band of superior beings ; it will be no more hierarchical than the art of past time was, but like it will be a gift of the people to the people, a thing which everybody can understand, and every one surround with love, it will be a part of every life, and a hindrance to none.

For this is the essence of art, and the thing that is eternal to it, whatever else may be passing and accidental.

Here it is, you see, wherein the art of to-day is so far astray, — would that I could say wherein it *has been* astray, — it has been sick because of this packing and peeling with tyranny, and now with what of life it has it must struggle back towards equality.

There is the hard business for us ! to get all simple people to care about art, to get them to insist on making it part of their lives, whatever becomes of systems of commerce and labor held perfect by some of us.

This is henceforward for a long time to come the real business of art: and — yes, I will say it since I think it, of civilization too for that matter : but how shall we set to work about it ? How shall we give people without traditions of art eyes with which to see the works we do to move them ? How shall we give them leisure from toil and truce with anxiety, so that they may have time to brood over

the longing for beauty which men are born with, as
't is said, even in London streets? And chiefly, for
this will breed the others swiftly and certainly, how
shall we give them hope and pleasure in their daily
work?

How shall we give them this soul of art without
which men are worse than savages? If they would
but drive us to it! But what and where are the
forces that shall drive them to drive us? Where
is the lever and the standpoint?

Hard questions indeed! but unless we are prepared to seek an answer for them, our art is a
mere toy, which may amuse us for a little, but
which will not sustain us at our need: the cultivated classes, as they are called, will feel it slipping
away from under them; till some of them will but
mock it as a worthless thing; and some will stand
by and look at it as a curious exercise of the
intellect, useless when done, though amusing to
watch a doing. How long will art live on those
terms? Yet such were even now the state of art
were it not for that hope which I am here to set
forth to you, the hope of an art that shall express
the soul of the people.

Therefore, I say, that in these days we men of
civilization have to choose if we will cast art aside
or not; if we choose to do so I have no more to
say, save that we *may* find something to take its
place for the solace and joy of mankind, but I
scarce think we shall: But if we refuse to cast art

aside then must we seek an answer for those hard questions aforesaid, of which this is the first?

How shall we set about giving people without traditions of art eyes with which to see works of art? It will doubtless take many years of striving and success, before we can think of answering that question fully: and if we strive to do our duty herein, long before it is answered fully there will be some kind of a popular art abiding among us : but meantime, and setting aside the answer which every artist must make to his own share of the question, there is one duty obvious to us all ; it is that we should set ourselves, each one of us, to doing our best to guard the natural beauty of the earth : we ought to look upon it as a crime, an injury to our fellows, only excusable because of ignorance, to mar that natural beauty, which is the property of all men ; and scarce less than a crime to look on and do nothing while others are marring it, if we can no longer plead this ignorance.

Now this duty, as it is the most obvious to us, and the first and readiest way of giving people back their eyes, so happily it is the easiest to set about ; up to a certain point you will have all people of good will to the public good on your side : nay, small as the beginning is, something has actually been begun in this direction, and we may well say, considering how hopeless things looked twenty years ago that it is marvellous in our eyes ! Yet if we ever get out of the troubles that we are now wallowing in, it will seem perhaps more marvellous still to those that come after us that the dwellers in the richest city in the world were at one time rather proud that the members of a small, humble, and rather obscure, though I will say it, a beneficent society, should have felt it their duty to shut their eyes to the apparent hopelessness of attacking with their feeble means the stupendous evils they had become alive to, so that they might be able to make some small beginnings towards awakening the general public to a due sense of those evils.   '

I say, that though I ask your earnest support for such associations as the Kyrle and the Commons Preservation Societies, and though I feel sure that they have begun at the right end, since neither gods nor governments will help those who don't themselves; though we are bound to wait for nobody's help than our own in dealing with the devouring hideousness and squalor of our great towns, and especially of London, for which the whole country is responsible; yet it would be idle not to acknowledge that the difficulties in our way are far too huge and wide-spreading to be grappled by private or semi-private efforts only.

All we can do in this way we must look on not as palliatives of an unendurable state of things but as tokens of what we desire; which is in short the giving back to our country of the natural beauty of the earth, which we are so ashamed of having taken away from it: and our chief duty herein will be to quicken this shame and the pain that comes from it in the hearts of our fellows: this I say is one of the chief duties of all those who have any right to the title of cultivated men: and I believe that if we are faithful to it, we may help to further a great impulse towards beauty among us, which will be so irresistible that it will fashion for itself a national machinery which will sweep away all difficulties between us and a decent life, though they may have increased a thousand-fold meantime, as is only too like to be the case.

Surely that light will arise, though neither we nor our children's children see it, though civilization may have to go down into dark places enough meantime: surely one day making will be thought more honorable, more worthy the majesty of a great nation, than destruction.

It is strange indeed, it is woful, it is scarcely comprehensible, if we come to think of it as men, and not as machines, that, after all the progress of civilization, it should be so easy for a little official talk, a few lines on a sheet of paper to set a terrible engine to work, which without any trouble on our part will slay us ten thousand men, and ruin who can say how many thousand of families ; and it lies light enough on the conscience of *all* of us ; while, if it is a question of striking a blow at grievous and crushing evils which lie at our own doors, evils which every thoughtful man feels and laments, and for which we alone are responsible, not only is there no national machinery for dealing with them, though they grow ranker and ranker every year, but any hint that such a thing may be possible is received with laughter or with terror, or with severe and heavy blame. The rights of property, the necessities of morality, the interests of religion — these are the sacramental words of cowardice that silence us !

Sirs, I have spoken of thoughtful men who feel these evils : but think of all the millions of men whom our civilization has bred, who are not thoughtful, and have had no chance of being so ; how can you fail then to acknowledge the duty of defending the fairness of the Earth ? and what is the use of our cultivation if it is to cultivate us into cowards ? Let us answer those feeble counsels of despair and say, we also have a property which your tyranny of squalor cheats us of ; we also have a morality which its baseness crushes ; we also have a religion which its injustice makes a mock of.

Well, whatever lesser helps there may be to our endeavor of giving people back the eyes we have robbed them of, we may pass them by at present, for they are chiefly of use to people who are beginning to get their eyesight again ; to people who, though they have no traditions of art, can study those mighty impulses that once led nations and races : it is to such that museums and art education are of service; but it is clear they cannot get at the great mass of people, who will at present stare at them in unintelligent wonder.

Until our streets are decent and orderly, and our town gardens break the bricks and mortar every here and there, and are open to all people ; until our meadows even near our towns become fair and sweet, and are unspoiled by patches of hideousness ; until we have clear sky above our heads and green grass beneath our feet ; until the great drama of the seasons can touch our workmen with other feelings than the misery of winter and the weariness of summer ; till all this happens our museums and art schools will be but amusements of the rich; and they will soon cease to be of any use to them also, unless they make up their minds that they will do their best to give us back the fairness of the Earth.

In what I have been saying on this last point I have been thinking of our own special duties as cultivated people, but in our endeavors towards this end, as in all others, cultivated people cannot stand alone ; nor can we do much to open people's eyes till they cry out to us to have them opened. Now I cannot doubt that the longing to attack and over-come the sordidness of the city life of to-day still dwells in the minds of workmen, as well as in ours, but it can scarcely be otherwise than vague and lacking guidance with men who have so little leisure, and are so hemmed in with hideousness as

they are.   So this brings us to our second question :
How shall people in general get leisure enough
from toil and truce enough with anxiety to give
scope to their inborn longing for beauty?

Now the part of this question that is not involved in the next one, How shall they get proper
work to do? is I think in a fair way to be answered.

The mighty change which the success of competitive commerce has wrought in the world, whatever it may have destroyed, has at least unwittingly
made one thing, — from out of it has been born the
increasing power of the working-class.   The determination which this power has bred in it to raise
their class as a class will I doubt not make way
and prosper with our good-will or even in spite of
it : but it seems to me that both to the working
class and especially to ourselves it is important that
it should have our abundant good-will, and also what
help we may be able otherwise to give it, by our
determination to deal fairly with workmen, even
when that justice may seem to involve our own
loss.   The time of unreasonable and blind outcry
against the Trades Unions is, I am happy to think,
gone by ; and has given place to the hope of a
time when these great Associations, well organized,
well served, and earnestly supported, as I *know*
them to be, will find other work before them than
the temporary support of their members and the
adjustment of due wages for their crafts : when

that hope begins to be realized, and they find they can make use of the help of us scattered units of the cultivated classes, I feel sure that the claims of art, as we and they will then understand the word, will by no means be disregarded by them.

Meantime with us who are called artists, since most unhappily that word means at present another thing than artisan : with us who either practise the arts with our own hands, or who love them so wholly that we can enter into the inmost feelings of those who do, — with us it lies to deal with our last question, to stir up others to think of answering this : How shall we give people in general hope and pleasure in their daily work in such a way that in those days to come the word art *shall* be rightly understood ?

Of all that I have to say to you this seems to me the most important, — that our daily and neces-sary work, which we could not escape if we would, which we would not forego if we could, should be human, serious, and pleasurable, not machine-like, trivial, or grievous. I call this not only the very foundation of Architecture in all senses of the word, but of happiness also in all conditions of life.

Let me say before I go further, that though I am nowise ashamed of repeating the words of men who have been before me in both senses, of time and insight I mean, I should be ashamed of letting you think that I forget their labors on which mine are founded. I know that the pith of what I am saying on this subject was set forth years ago and for the first time by Mr. Ruskin in that chapter of the Stones of Venice, which is entitled, ' On the Nature of Gothic,' in words more clear and eloquent than any man else now living could use. So important do they seem to me that to my mind they should have been posted up in every school of art throughout the country; nay, in every association of English-speaking people which professes in any way to further the culture of mankind. But I am sorry to have to say it, my excuse for doing little more now than repeating those words is that they have been less heeded than most things which Mr. Ruskin has said : I suppose because people have been afraid of them, lest they should find the truth they express sticking so fast in their minds that it would either compel them to act on it, or confess themselves slothful and cowardly.

Nor can I pretend to wonder at that: for if people were once to accept it as true, that it is nothing but just and fair that every man's work should have some hope and pleasure always present in it, they must try to bring the change about that would make it so : and all history tells of no greater change in man's life than that would be.

Nevertheless, great as the change may be, Architecture has no prospects in civilization unless the change be brought about : and 't is my business to-day, I will not say to convince you of this, but to send some of you away uneasy lest perhaps it may be true; if I can manage that I shall have spoken to some purpose.

Let us see however in what light cultivated people, men not without serious thoughts about life, look at this matter, lest perchance we may seem to be beating the air only: when I have given you an example of this way of thinking, I will answer it to the best of my power, in the hopes of making some of you uneasy discontented and revolutionary.

Some few months ago I read in a paper the report of a speech made to the assembled work-people of a famous firm of manufacturers (as they are called). The speech was a very humane and thoughtful one, spoken by one of the leaders of modern thought: the firm to whose people it was addressed was and is famous not only for successful commerce but also for the consideration and good will with which it treats its work-people, men and women. No wonder, therefore, that the speech was pleasant reading; for the tone of it was that of a man speaking to his friends who could well understand him and from whom he need hide nothing; but toward the end of it I came across a sentence, which set me a-thinking so hard, that I forgot all that had gone before. It was to this effect, and I think nearly in these very words, 'Since no man would work if it were not that he hoped by working to earn leisure': and the context showed that this was assumed as a self-evident truth.

Well, for many years I have had my mind fixed
on what I in my turn regarded as an axiom which
may be worded thus ; No work which cannot be
done without pleasure in the doing is worth doing ;
so you may think I was much disturbed at a grave
and learned man taking such a completely different
view of it with such calmness of certainty. What
a little way, I thought, has all Ruskin's fire and eloquence made in driving into people so great a truth,
a truth so fertile of consequences !

Then I turned the intrusive sentence over again
in my mind : 'No man would work unless he hoped
by working to earn leisure :' and I saw that this
was another way of putting it : first, all the work of
the world is done against the grain : second, what
a man does in his 'leisure' is not work.

A poor bribe the hope of such leisure to supple-
ment the other inducement to toil, which I take to
be the fear of death by starvation : a poor bribe ;
for the most of men like those Yorkshire weavers
and spinners (and the more part far worse than
they) work for such a very small share of leisure
that one must needs say that if all their hope be
in that, they are pretty much beguiled of their
hope !

So I thought, and this next, that if it were indeed true and beyond remedy, that no man would
work unless he hoped by working to earn leisure,
the hell of theologians was but little needed; for
a thickly populated civilized country, where, you

know, after all people must work at something, would serve their turn well enough. Yet again I knew that this theory of the general and necessary hatefulness of work was indeed the common one, and that all sorts of people held it, who without being monsters of insensibility grew fat and jolly nevertheless.

So to explain this puzzle, I fell to thinking of the one life of which I knew something — my own to wit — and out tumbled the bottom of the theory.

For I tried to think what would happen to me if I were forbidden my ordinary daily work ; and I knew that I should die of despair and weariness, unless I could straightway take to something else which I could make my daily work : and it was clear to me that I worked not in the least in the world for the sake of earning leisure by it, but partly driven by the fear of starvation or disgrace, and partly, and even a very great deal, because I love the work itself : and as for my leisure : well I had to confess that part of it I do indeed spend as a dog does — in contemplation, let us say ; and like it well enough : but part of it also I spend in work : which work gives me just as much pleasure as my bread earning work — neither more nor less ; and therefore could be no bribe or hope for my work-a-day hours.

Then next I turned my thoughts to my friends : mere artists, and therefore, you know, lazy people by prescriptive right : I found that the one thing

they enjoyed was their work, and that their only
idea of happy leisure was other work, just as valuable to the world as their work-a-day work: they
only differed from me in liking the dog-like leisure
less and the man-like labor more than I do.

I got no further when I turned from mere artists,
to important men — public men: I could see no
signs of their working merely to earn leisure: they
all worked for the work and the deeds' sake. Do
rich gentlemen sit up all night in the House of
Commons for the sake of earning leisure? if so,
't is a sad waste of labor. Or Mr. Gladstone? he
does n't seem to have succeeded in winning much
leisure by tolerably strenuous work ; what he does
get he might have got on much easier terms, I am
sure.

Does it then come to this, that there are men,
say a class of men, whose daily work, though maybe they cannot escape from doing it, is chiefly
pleasure to them ; and other classes of men
whose daily work is wholly irksome to them,
and only endurable because they hope while they
are about it to earn thereby a little leisure at the
day's end?

If that were wholly true the contrast between
the two kinds of lives would be greater than the
contrast between the utmost delicacy of life and the
utmost hardship could show, or between the utmost
calm and the utmost trouble. The difference would
be literally immeasurable.

But I dare not, if I would, in so serious a matter overstate the evils I call on you to attack : it is not wholly true that such immeasurable difference exists between the lives of divers classes of men, or the world would scarce have got through to past the middle of this century : misery, grudging, and tyranny would have destroyed us all.

The inequality even at the worst is not really so great as that : any employment in which a thing can be done better or worse has some pleasure in it, for all men do more or less like doing what they can do well : even mechanical labor is pleasant to some people (to me amongst others) if it be not too mechanical.

Nevertheless though it be not wholly true that the daily work of some men is merely pleasant and of others merely grievous : yet is it over true both that things are not very far short of this, and also that if people do not open their eyes in time they will speedily worsen ? Some work, nay, almost all the work done by artisans *is* too mechanical ; and those that work at it must either abstract their thoughts from it altogether, in which case they are but machines while they are at work ; or else they must suffer such dreadful weariness in getting through it, as one can scarcely bear to think of. Nature, who desires that we shall at least live, but seldom, I suppose, allows this latter misery to happen ; and the workmen who do purely mechanical work do as a rule become mere machines as far

as their work is concerned. Now as I am quite
sure that no art, not even the feeblest rudest or
least intelligent, can come of such work, so also I
am sure that such work makes the workman less
than a man and degrades him grievously and unjustly, and that nothing can compensate him or us
for such degradation : and I want you specially to
note that this was instinctively felt in the very
earliest days of what are called the industrial arts.
When a man turned the wheel, or threw the shuttle,
or hammered the iron, he was expected to make
something more than a water-pot, a cloth, or a
knife : he was expected to make a work of art
also : he could scarcely altogether fail in this, he
might attain to making a work of the greatest
beauty : this was felt to be positively necessary to
the peace of mind both of the maker and the user ;
and this it is which I have called Architecture :
the turning of necessary articles of daily use into
works of art.

Certainly, when we come to think of it thus,
there does seem to be little less than that immeasurable contrast above mentioned between such work
and mechanical work : and most assuredly do I
believe that the crafts which fashion our familiar
wares need this enlightenment of happiness no less
now than they did in the days of the early Pharaohs
but we have forgotten this necessity, and in consequence have reduced handicraft to such degradation,
that a learned, thoughtful and humane man can set

forth as an axiom that no man will work except to earn leisure thereby.

But now let us forget any conventional ways of looking at the labor which produces the matters of our daily life, which ways come partly from the wretched state of the arts in modern times, and partly I suppose from that repulsion to handicraft which seems to have beset some minds in all ages : let us forget this, and try to think how it really fares with the divers ways of work in handicrafts.

I think one may divide the work with which Architecture is conversant into three classes : first there is the purely mechanical : those who do this are machines only, and the less they think of what they are doing the better for the purpose, supposing they are properly drilled : the purpose of this work, to speak plainly, is not the making of wares of any kind, but what on the one hand is called employment, on the other what is called money-making · that is to say, in other words, the multiplication of the species of the mechanical workman, and the increase of the riches of the man who sets him to work, called in our modern jargon by a strange perversion of language, a manufacturer : Let us call this kind of work Mechanical Toil.

The second kind is more or less mechanical as the case may be ; but it can always be done better or worse : if it is to be well done, it claims attention from the workman, and he must leave on it signs of his individuality : there will be more or less of art in it, over which the workman has had at least some control ; and he will work on it partly to earn his bread in not too toilsome or disgusting a way, but in a way which makes even his work-hours pass pleasantly to him, and partly to make wares, which when made will be a distinct gain to the world ; things that will be praised and delighted in. This work I would call Intelligent Work.

The third kind of work has but little if anything mechanical about it ; it is altogether individual ; that is to say, that what any man does by means of it could never have been done by any other man. Properly speaking, this work is all pleasure : true, there are pains and perplexities and wearinesses in it, but they are like the troubles of a beautiful life ; the dark places that make the bright ones brighter : they are the romance of the work and do but elevate the workman, not depress him : I would call this Imaginative Work.

Now I can fancy that at first sight it may seem to you as if there were more difference between this last and Intelligent Work, than between Intelligent Work and Mechanical Toil : but 't is not so. The difference between these two is the difference between light and darkness, between Ormusd and Ahriman : whereas the difference between Intelligent work and what for want of a better word I am calling Imaginative work, is a matter of degree only ; and in times when art is abundant and noble there is no break in the chain from the humblest of the lower to the greatest of the higher class : from the poor weaver who chuckles as the bright color comes round again, to the great painter anxious and doubtful if he can give to the world the whole of his thought or only nine-tenths of it, they are all artists — that is men ; while the mechanical work-man, who does not note the difference between bright and dull in his colors, but only knows them by numbers, is, while he is at his work, no man, but a machine. Indeed when Intelligent work coexists with Imaginative, there is no hard and fast line between them ; in the very best and happiest times of art, there is scarce any Intelligent work which is not Imaginative also ; and there is but little of effort or doubt or sign of unexpressed desires even in the highest of the Imaginative work : the blessing of Equality elevates the lesser, and calms the greater art.

Now further, Mechanical Toil is bred of that hurry and thoughtlessness of civilization of which, as aforesaid, the middle-classes of this country have been such powerful furtherers : on the face of it it is hostile to civilization, a curse that civiliza-tion has made for itself and can no longer think of abolishing or controlling : such it seems, I say, but since it bears with it change and tremendous change, it may well be that there is something more than mere loss in it : it will full surely destroy art as we know art, unless art newborn destroy it : yet belike at the worst it will destroy other things beside which are the poison of art, and in the long run itself also, and thus make way for the new art, of whose form we know nothing.

Intelligent work is the child of struggling, hopeful, progressive civilization : and its office is to add fresh interest to simple and uneventful lives, to soothe discontent with innocent pleasure fertile of deeds gainful to mankind ; to bless the many toiling millions with hope daily recurring, and which it will by no means disappoint.

Imaginative work is the very blossom of civilization triumphant and hopeful ; it would fain lead men to aspire towards perfection : each hope that it fulfils gives birth to yet another hope : it bears in its bosom the worth and the meaning of life and the counsel to strive to understand everything, to fear nothing and to hate nothing : in a word 't is the symbol and sacrament of the Courage of the World.

Now thus it stands to-day with these three kinds of work : Mechanical Toil has swallowed Intelligent Work and all the lower part of Imaginative Work, and the enormous mass of the very worst now confronts the slender but still bright array of the very best : what is left of art is rallied to its citadel of the highest intellectual art, and stands at bay there.

At first sight its hope of victory is slender indeed : yet to us now living it seems as if man had

not yet lost all that part of his soul which longs
for beauty : nay we cannot but hope that it is not
yet dying. If we are not deceived in that hope, if
the art of to-day has really come alive out of the
slough of despond which we call the eighteenth
century, it will surely grow and gather strength,
and draw to it other forms of intellect and hope
that now scarcely know it; and then, whatever
changes it may go through, it will at the last be
victorious, and bring abundant content to mankind.
On the other hand, if, as some think, it be but the
reflection and feeble ghost of that glorious autumn
which ended the good days of the mighty art of
the Middle Ages, it will take but little killing :
Mechanical Toil will sweep over all the handiwork
of man, and art will be gone.

I myself am too busy a man to trouble myself
much as to what may happen after that : I can
only say that if you do not like the thought of that
dull blank, even if you know or care little for art,
do not cast the thought of it aside, but think of it'
again and again, and cherish the trouble it breeds
till such a future seems unendurable to you ; and
then make up your minds that you will not bear it ;
and, even if you distrust the artists that now are,
set yourself to clear the way for the artists that
are to come. We shall not count you among our
enemies then, however hardly you deal with us.

I have spoken of one most important part of
that task ; I have prayed you to set yourselves

earnestly to protecting what is left, and recovering what is lost of the Natural Fairness of the Earth: no less I pray you to do what you may to raise up some firm ground amid the great flood of mechanical toil, to make an effort to win human and hopeful work for yourselves and your fellows.

But if our first task of guarding the beauty of the Earth was hard, this is far harder, nor can I pretend to think that we can attack our enemy directly; yet indirectly surely something may be done, or at least the foundations laid for something.

For Art breeds Art, and every worthy work done and delighted in by maker and user begets a longing for more: and since art cannot be fashioned by mechanical toil, the demand for real art will mean a demand for intelligent work, which if persisted in will in time create its due supply — at least I hope so.

I believe that what I am now saying will be well understood by those who really care about art, but to speak plainly I know that these are rarely to be found even among the cultivated classes: it must be confessed that the middle classes of our civilization have embraced luxury instead of art, and that we are even so blindly base as to hug ourselves on it, and to insult the memory of valiant peoples of past times and to mock at them because they were not encumbered with the nuisances that foolish habit has made us look on as necessaries. Be sure that

we are not beginning to prepare for the art that is
to be, till we have swept all that out of our minds,
and are setting to work to rid ourselves of all
the useless luxuries (by some called comforts) that
make our stuffy art-stifling houses more truly sav
age than a Zulu's kraal or an East Greenlander's
snow hut.

I feel sure that many a man is longing to set his
hand to this if he only durst; I believe that there
are simple people who. think that they are dull to
art, and who are really only perplexed and wearied
by finery and rubbish : if not from these, 't is at
least from the children of these that we may look
for the beginnings of the building up of the art
that is to be.

Meanwhile, I say, till the beginning of new con-
struction is obvious, let us be at least destructive
of the sham art : it is full surely one of the curses
of modern life, that if people have not time and
eyes to discern or money to buy the real object of
their desire, they must needs have its mechanical
substitute. On this lazy and cowardly habit feeds
and grows and flourishes mechanical toil and all
the slavery of mind and body it brings with it ·
from this stupidity are born the itch of the public
to over-reach the tradesmen they deal with, the
determination (usually successful) of the tradesman
to over-reach them, and all the mockery and flout-
ing that has been cast of late (not without reason)
on the British tradesman and the British work-

man, — men just as honest as ourselves, if we would not compel them to cheat us, and reward them for doing it.

Now if the public knew anything of art, that is excellence in things made by man, they would not abide the shams of it ; and if the real thing were not to be had, they would learn to do without, nor think their gentility injured by the forbearance.

Simplicity of life, even the barest, is not misery, but the very foundation of refinement : a sanded floor and whitewashed walls, and the green trees, and flowery meads, and living waters outside ; or a grimy palace amid the smoke with a regiment of housemaids always working to smear the dirt together so that it may be unnoticed ; which, think you, is the most refined, the most fit for a gentleman of those two dwellings ?

So I say, if you cannot learn to love real art, at least learn to hate sham art and reject it. It is not so much because the wretched thing is so ugly and silly and useless that I ask you to cast it from you ; it is much more because these are but the outward symbols of the poison that lies within them : look through them and see all that has gone to their fashioning, and you will see how vain labor, and sorrow, and disgrace have been their companions from the first, — and all this for trifles that no man really needs !

Learn to do without ; there is virtue in those words ; a force that rightly used would choke both demand and supply of Mechanical Toil: would make it stick to its last : the making of machines.

And then from simplicity of life would rise up the longing for beauty, which cannot yet be dead in men's souls, and we know that nothing can satisfy that demand but Intelligent work rising gradually into Imaginative work ; which will turn all 'operatives' into workmen, into artists, into men.

Now, I have been trying to show you how the hurry of Modern Civilization accompanied by the tyrannous organization of labor which was a necessity to the full development of Competitive Commerce, has taken from the people at large, gentle and simple, the eyes to discern and the hands to fashion that popular art which was once the chief solace and joy of the world : I have asked you to think of that as no light matter but a grievous mishap: I have prayed you to strive to remedy this evil: first by guarding jealously what is left, and by trying earnestly to win back what is lost of the Fairness of the Earth ; and next by rejecting luxury, that you may embrace art, if you can, or if indeed you in your short lives cannot learn what art means, that you may at least live a simple life fit for men.

And in all I have been saying, what I have been really urging on you is this ; Reverence for the life of Man upon the Earth : let the past be past, every whit of it that is not still living in us : let the dead bury their dead, but let us turn to the living, and with boundless courage and what hope we may, refuse to let the Earth be joyless in the days to come.

What lies before us of hope or fear for this? Well, let us remember that those past days whose art was so worthy, did nevertheless forget much of what was due to the Life of Man upon the Earth ; and so belike it was to revenge this neglect that art was delivered to our hands for maiming : to us, who were blinded by our eager chase of those things which our forefathers had neglected, and by the chase of other things which seemed revealed to us on our hurried way, not seldom, it may be for our beguiling.

And of that to which we were blinded, not all was unworthy: nay the most of it was deep-rooted in men's souls, and was a necessary part of their Life upon the Earth, and claims our reverence still : let us add this knowledge to our other knowledge, and there will still be a future for the arts. Let us remember this, and amid simplicity of life turn our eyes to real beauty that can be shared by all : and then though the days worsen, and no rag of the elder art be left for our teaching, yet the new art may yet arise among us : and even if it have the hands of a child together with the heart of a troubled man, still it may bear on for us to better times the tokens of our reverence for the Life of Man upon the Earth.   For we indeed freed from the bondage of foolish habit and dulling luxury might at last have eyes wherewith to see: and should have to babble to one another many things of our joy in the life around us: the faces of people in the streets bearing the tokens of mirth and sorrow and hope, and all the tale of their lives: the scraps of nature the busiest of us would come across ; birds and beasts and the little worlds they live in ; and even in the very town the sky above us and the drift of the clouds across it ; the wind's hand on the slim trees, and its voice amid their branches, and all the ever-recurring deeds of nature nor would the road or the river winding past our homes fail to tell us stories of the country-side, and men's doings in field and fell. And whiles we should fall to muse on the times when all the ways of nature were mere wonders to men, yet so well beloved of them that they called them by men's names and gave them deeds of men to do: and many a time there would come before us memories of the deeds of past times, and of the aspirations of those mighty peoples whose deaths have made our lives, and their sorrows our joys.

How could we keep silence of all this? and what voice could tell it but the voice of art: and what audience for such a tale would content us but all men living on the Earth?

This is what Architecture hopes to be: it will have this life, or else death ; and it is for us now living between the past and the future to say whether it shall live or die.

The House of the Wolfings. A Tale of the House of the Wolfings and all the Kindreds of the Mark. Written in Prose and in Verse. 12mo. $2.00.

The story, which is in a strong Homeric vein that immediately commands and holds attention, takes us back to those far-off times when the Goths were contending with the Romans. It is written in both prose and verse, and is thereby made mcre continuously interesting for the general reader than if it were a purely epic poem. It relates to a branch of the Gothic family who exhibited, particularly in their leader, Thiodolf, many noble examples of heroism and self-sacrifice. The narrative is pathetic, inspiring, and worthy of the author of "The Earthly Paradise," and recalls a far-distant past with a picturesque fidelity that is far more impressive than the bald realism which too many believe now to be the highest art in story-telling It has an imaginative fervor, glow, and color which will cause it to be read and re-read by those who wish to escape from the present into a world of romance and poetry. This literary jewel, with its rich and appropriate setting, should be in the library of every genuine book-lover. — *Saturday Evening Gazette.*

The Story of the Glittering Plain. Which has been also called the Land of Living Men, or the Acre of the Undying. $1.50.

William Morris comes to us again with another of his delightful "sagas," full of life and action and every essential human sentiment. He is a master of such production, and does not betray himself at any point by a false note or by false color. . . . The saga before us contains a story of happy life and prospective wedded joy broken in upon by capture, of a long and varied search for his loved one by the knight of the tale, of successful return from all dangers, and a final re-entrance into the hall of the kindred in "Cleveland by the Sea." . . . This saga sings itself through from beginning to end in a beautiful melody. The prose of it is like music, and the little interludes of song fit their places perfectly. The human life and circumstances of the saga are drawn from ancient Northern times, though no definite sphere is entered; and there is no attempt at historical suggestion, as in "The House of the Wolfings." This is simply a sweet, touching saga of a brave, patient, faithful human love. — *Public Opinion.*

Poems by the Way. 12mo. $1.25.

Those who feared that Mr. William Morris would be made less of a poet by his socialism have had ample reason to be disappointed. . . . The originality of this volume is that it contains several poems telling us something which Mr. Morris has hardly told us in print before. . . . The whole volume not only betokens a splendid vitality of gift with surprises yet in store, but recalls at every turn that its author is one of a famous fraternity, of whom one other still survives, and who have been animated, despite all their differences, by a certain common spirit, and endowed with a similar cunning in the craft of song. — *The Academy.*

The Wood Beyond the World. In a crown 8vo volume, printed on antique English paper, with decorative cover. Frontispiece by E. Burne-Jones. $2.50.

The charm, or one of the charms, of this last book of his is more easily felt than described, and is only felt in the feelings, we think, by those who are enamoured of the invention which underlies all folk-lore, the element of fantasy, with or without a seeming purpose, containing in itself its excuse for being, and are enamoured at the same time of the simple, homely, idiomatic diction which characterized the early chroniclers and romancers, and of which Malory's "Morte d'Arthur" is a fair example. At the age of sixty, or thereabouts, he is still pouring out his lovely things, more full of the glory of youth, more full of romantic adventure and romantic love, than any of the beautiful poems in his first volume. By the side of this exhaustless creator of youthful and lovely things, the youngest of the poets who have just appeared above the horizon seems faded and jaded. — *Mail and Express.*

LONGMANS, GREEN & CO., PUBLISHERS,

91 AND 93 FIFTH AVENUE, NEW YORK.

CPSIA information can be obtained at www.ICGtesting.com
Printed in the USA
BVOW05s0725281115

428725BV00038B/767/P